THE OFFICIAL
HIGH TIMES®
FIELD GUIDE TO
MARIJUANA
STRAINS

The Official HIGH TIMES Field Guide to Marijuana Strains

By Danny Danko
Senior Cultivation Editor, HIGH TIMES Magazine

HIGH TIMES BOOKS

Produced by HIGH TIMES Books

Publisher: Mary McEvoy
Business Manager: Michael Safir
Art Director: Elise McDonough
Managing Editor: Natasha Lewin
Copy Editor: Rick Szykowny
Proofreader: Mary Jane Gibson
Cover Photos: Andre Grossmann, Danny Danko, HT Archive
Back Cover Photos: South Bay Ray, Murphy Green

First Edition: November 2010
Second Printing: April 2011

ISBN #: 1-893010-28-4
Price: $14.95

PRINTED IN CANADA

Dedication

In honor of all the marijuana breeders, past and present, who did the work and took the risks to keep great pot varieties alive and preserve wonderful ganja genetics for future generations to medicate with and enjoy. And for the countless POW growers behind bars, whose lives were disrupted at best—and ruined at worst—by the misguided policies of the War on Flowers. We will never forget your sacrifices.

Table of Contents

Danny and Jorge conduct a tasting.

Foreword

By Jorge Cervantes

Danny Danko and I have worked together for almost a decade. Side by side, we've shot photos at the HIGH TIMES Cannabis Cup in Amsterdam, toured gardens in Europe, appeared on radio shows and at marijuana conferences, and—naturally—we've medicated together many, many times while contemplating the local strains wherever we happened to be at the time. After getting to know Danny, I realized he was the only choice to take over my question-and-answer cultivation column in HIGH TIMES. And after reading his columns each month for more than a year, I'm 100 percent convinced that I made the right decision.

So you can imagine my delight at learning that Danny has now compiled another aspect of his knowledge into this very useful book for growers and connoisseurs alike!

After helping to judge the HIGH TIMES Cannabis Cup in Amsterdam for many years, Danny has an uncanny ability to evaluate cannabis's many unique varieties, and a deep knowledge of their various lineages. He also knows many of the top breeders and seed developers personally, which gives him rare insight into this industry.

Although Danny's tastes run toward the classics, his book includes a complete selection of strains with different characteristics and growth habits from around the world. He also keeps his taste buds tuned to the newest cannabis varieties you need to know about, which often earn a spot in his annual "Top 10 Strains of the Year" feature in HIGH TIMES.

In this excellent field guide, Danny's years of experience translate into easy-to-reference information on more than 125 strains, all at the flip of a finger, condensing everything you need to know into one concise, in-depth, easy-to-read package—with great photos, too!

Written from a grower's perspective, Danko gives specific cultivation details on each strain. The text is complete and very well researched. His practical approach makes it easy to sort through the strains and choose the ones that are best for your needs.

All of which means, if you're like me, you'll want to keep a copy of *The Official HIGH TIMES Field Guide to Marijuana Strains* close at hand during all of your cannabis adventures.

Introduction

When most people find out what I do for a living, one of the first questions they ask is whether I can truly tell the difference between various strains of pot. Some of these folks are daily pot smokers, and I'm often taken aback by the implications inherent in their inquiry—that all cannabis is pretty much the same, and that I'm engaged in some form of delusion or snobbery when I seek to quantify the differences.

In the rarefied world of pot connoisseurship, we hold these truths to be self-evident: that all strains are *not* created equal, that an *indica*-dominant and stony Afghani Hash Plant is worlds apart from a Cambodian Haze with extreme *sativa*-like characteristics. We dissect the intensity and effects of the highs, preferring one variety for a daytime smoke and another one entirely for a nightcap.

Flavors, colors and scents all play a role in our appreciation (or disdain) for a certain strain. We even consider *terroir*, the distinct characteristics bestowed by soil and geography. Organic and even biodynamic growing methods and pest control are as essential to our enjoyment of the final product as how it looks under a microscope or loupe.

We, the cannabis consumers of the world, are getting pretty picky about what we'll smoke or vaporize, and growers and breeders have a hard time keeping up with our desires. A few years ago, *indicas* were all the rage, and everyone was looking for stocky, short-flowering plants to grow "sea of green" (SOG) style. Recently, *sativas* have gained prominence, and "screen of green" (ScrOG) methods were employed to keep them from stretching to the ceiling. In some places, people love the purple-colored varieties, while in others, aficionados only smoke the Kush.

It can be hard keeping track of all the new varieties on the ever-changing market. That's why I decided to write this book. Several wonderful coffee-table books on pot varieties already exist, but I've never seen something like a field guide. This is a book you can take along in your back pocket while traveling in Amsterdam, Vancouver, Spain or Burlington, VT. With over 125 strains listed, my hope is that readers will become inspired to smoke or vaporize every single one.

You can even call us "pot snobs" if you wish. We'll wear that label with pride.—**Danny Danko**

How to Use This Book

Each page describes a marijuana variety with as much relevant information as it was possible to gather on its genetic heritage and growing habits. Flavors, scents and the experience of its effects are all listed and described. All flowering times given are for indoor growing unless otherwise indicated, and contact information is included where relevant.

In cases where the lineage is known, it's given with the male parent listed first (male x female: e.g., Mazar x Trainwreck). When the lineage is unknown, as much available information as possible is provided. When hybrids were crossed with hybrids, they are given with the parents listed in brackets: for example, [Afghani x Kush] x [Hawaiian x Nigerian].

Some terms you'll need to know:

Cultivar: A plant variety that's been selected for desirable traits.

F1: The F1 or Filial 1 hybrid is the result of the first cross of two plainly different parents (ie. a pure *indica* x pure *sativa*). These crosses typically result in hybrid vigor.

F2: A less consistent result of pollination of an F1 whose genetics will vary from good to useless.

Genotype: A particular inherited characteristic or trait (genotype + environment = phenotype).

Hybrid: The offspring of two distinct varieties or lines.

Hybrid Vigor: also known as Heterosis, F1 crosses with hybrid vigor improve on the genetics of their parent strains by growing stronger and quicker.

Inbred Lines (IBLs): Genetically stable representations of a specific landrace.

Landrace: A strain that has adapted over generations to its climate and environment. Landraces show more diversity than IBLs.

Phenotype: The visible genetic expression produced by hybrids in their environment (i.e., a *sativa*-dominant or *indica*-dominant phenotype of a particular hybrid strain can be produced from the same batch of seeds).

Chinese landrace.

Sativas stretch outdoors... and inside.

Heirloom Varieties

The building blocks of today's hybrids are the strains of yesteryear. These landraces are native to their growing region and have been acclimated and developed over centuries. Cannabis is thought to have originated in the Yunnan province of China and then was spread throughout the world by traders on the Silk Road.

Sativas are native to the Indian subcontinent, but are also grown in Southeast Asia, South and Central America, the Caribbean and Africa. Among the many landrace *sativas* from Southeast Asia are Lowland and Highland Thai, Vietnamese, Burmese, Cambodian and Laotian. Central and South American *sativas* include Panama Red, Acapulco Gold, Oaxacan Highland, Zacatecas Purple, Santa Marta Gold, Punta Roja and Brazilian. *Sativas* from the African continent include Malawi Gold, Durban Poison, Nigerian, Swazi Red, Swazi Skunk and Congolese. Hawaiian varieties such as Maui Wowie and Kona Gold round out the list.

Indicas were acclimated to the mountainous Hindu Kush region and are typically thought of as Afghani, Kashmiri or Kush. Asian *indica*-dominant strains include Hindu Kush, Mazar-i-Sharif, South Indian Kerala, Chitrali, Taskenti, Nepalese Highland, Pakistani and Uzbek. In the Middle East, Lebanese Hash Plant as well as Syrian and Egyptian strains are the traditional hash-making landrace varieties.

Early Hybrids: '70s, '80s and '90s

In the 1970s, wanderers returning to California and the Pacific Northwest from the "Hippie Trail" brought home seeds from India, Afghanistan and Southeast Asia. American bud-breeding experiments began in earnest with the new *indica*-dominant varieties, allowing the plants to finish in time to harvest before frosts. Some entrepreneurs ventured into the seed business, and many fled with their genetics to the relative safety of Amsterdam in the Netherlands.

Using original landrace seeds, bud-breeding pioneers such as Nevil Schoenbottom from the Seed Bank/Super Sativa Seed Club (SSSC), Sam Skunkman and Eddie from Sacred Seeds/Cultivator's Choice, and Ben Dronkers from Sensi Seed Bank created the first modern cannabis hybrids available to the general public. They crossed males and females of distinctly differing varieties (i.e., *sativa* x *indica*), resulting in F1 seeds exhibiting hybrid vigor, such as the Skunk #1, Skunk #5, Northern Lights, Original Haze, Hindu Kush, William's Wonder, G-13 and M-39. These strains became the basis for many of the varieties described in this book.

Dried Dalat colas.

Vietnamese Dalat.

Kush in the Indian Himalayas.

Life is full of interesting choices.

Cannabis Buyer's Guide

Which Strain Is Right for You?

For the millions of marijuana users living in states that in no way protect their rights, the black market offers several risks in addition to its rewards. Patients forced to break the law and buy from a "dealer" typically have little or no choice among strains when it comes time to make a purchase, let alone access to accurate information about what type of cannabis they're buying, or how it was cultivated.

Many black-market growers and dealers are highly ethical individuals, but the lack of a regulated system of distribution creates unnecessary risks for those with the poor fortune to live in states still hell-bent on prosecuting cancer patients for consuming personal amounts of cannabis on their doctor's recommendation.

The good news is that, if you're a licensed medical-marijuana patient, you're no longer subject to the vagaries of the black market. Instead, prepare to enter a bold new world of cannabis connoisseurship. First and foremost, you'll want to investigate all the different cannabis strains available, with an eye toward identifying the ones that are best suited to treating your particular malady.

Wide *indica* leaves. | Long and thin *sativa* leaves.

Indica and Sativa

In the broadest sense, cannabis breaks down into two fairly easily distinguishable lines, with *sativas* growing wild in almost all the equatorial regions of the globe, and *indicas* hailing from Asia and the Indian subcontinent.

Bred for centuries to make the world's best hashish, *indicas* grow short and stocky, maturing quickly and producing heavy buds coated in resin. In addition to THC, *indicas* produce high levels of a cannabinoid called CBD, which accounts for *indica's* heavy, "stony" effects. Kush varietals, which originated in the Hindu Kush region of Afghanistan (primarily), are an excellent example of a largely *indica*-dominant strain.

Sativas, on the other hand, grow as tall as 14 feet, take a long time to mature, and produce thin leaves and wispy buds. *Sativas* also produce a larger percentage of THC, accounting for their clear, soaring high. In this era of high-bred herb, it's rare to find a pure *sativa* on the market, but anyone who remembers Panama Red, Santa Marta Gold or Thai Stick will know what I'm talking about.

Nowadays, most strains are generally a hybridized combination of *indica* and *sativa*, hopefully incorporating the best traits of each. Given the largely underground nature of cannabis genetics, confusion can often get the best of even the savviest medical patient, never mind the uninitiated. So start your search for the perfect strain by finding a legally operating medical-marijuana supplier or, if growing your own, a seed company with a good reputation and knowledgeable staff—and then don't be afraid to ask questions.

Look Before You Leap

When it comes to cannabis, looks can definitely be deceiving. Marijuana bred for "bag appeal" doesn't always prove as potent or enjoyable as a less visually appealing alternative. Start by making sure the buds under consideration were harvested at their peak. Examine the glandular trichomes (or crystals) on the surface—with a microscope or loupe, if possible—to ensure that they're intact, plentiful, and

somewhere between clear and amber in color.

Next, examine the interior of the bud to make sure that it's free of mold, fungus and insect infestation. Buds should also have been properly dried and cured. Medicinal-grade buds should feel like cotton candy— sticky and squishy. A delicately handled, uniformly beautiful display of perfect little nuggets indicates medicine that has reached its full potential.

Don't Panic if It's Organic

Many top dispensaries and coffeeshops offer organically grown cannabis these days, and if you're concerned about potential residue from synthetic fertilizers and pesticides, you should definitely investigate the organic alternative. In the past few years, certification programs like Clean Green—run by USDA-licensed organic certifier and lawyer Chris Van Hook—have sprouted up to offer a parallel certification program for organic ganja, providing an incentive for growers and third-party verification for dispensaries and patients.

Environmentally-minded patients may also choose to support outdoor growers as a "green" alternative to the large carbon footprint of indoor growing. Keep in mind that since outdoor plants require no artificial high-intensity lights—and since they breathe in carbon dioxide and release oxygen—an outdoor sack of homegrown can theoretically have a *negative* carbon footprint. Also, don't believe the hype: Well-grown outdoor marijuana can be every bit as potent as indoor.

Savor the entire experience of partaking in cannabis.

The Nose Knows

Aromas can be extremely evocative, which means there's a good chance that if you really like the way a particular strain smells, it's because the scent reminds you of something you've responded well to in the past. But smells can be deceiving, too: Some of the best and most potent medical marijuana will have an acrid or even straw-like scent, while other strains will have little to no scent at all.

However, always beware of anything that smells too "green" or even moldy, as this is a sign that the bud has been improperly dried and cured.

High, How Are You?

Ultimately, when it comes to marijuana, looks, smell and genetic pedigree all give way to the most important consideration: How does ingesting this particular strain of cannabis make you feel? Nothing could be more personal or subjective than trying to explain your preference for one type of pot over another.

It certainly helps to take notes on each strain you sample, or at least take note of the ones you find most medically beneficial. In time, your appreciation for the subtle differences will grow—but even if you do eventually settle on a favorite strain, you may find that occasionally varying your herb of choice will help prevent building up a tolerance to your main strain's best effects.

Set the Mood

Find a safe place to toke, and always use clean paraphernalia or some nice thin papers of your choice. (Also, vaporizers work wonderfully for tasting all the complex flavors of cannabis.) Check the visuals and be sure to note how the bud looks: Was it hastily trimmed and dried? Pinch a bud and take a sniff—or, better yet, grind it up and then allow the aroma to waft over you. Examine the color of the cannabis: Is it light green, dark green or purple? Take a "dry toke" off your joint before lighting it: Does it taste the same as it smells? Keep a pen and paper handy for note-taking if you wish. Now you're ready to light up and enjoy!

Cannabis
Strains
A to Z

Lineage:
Pure Afghani back-crossed from Sensi's finest *indica* parent cultivars

Flowering Time:
6 to 7 weeks

Contact:
Sensi Seed Bank, sensiseeds.com

Afghani #1 • Sensi Seed Bank

It's fitting that we start with the Afghani #1, as it's an essential building block in so many breeding projects. Pure *indicas* such as the "Affy" changed the course of cannabis cultivation forever with their short flowering times, and their ability to withstand the harsh elements of mountainous regions such as western Canada and the northeastern US.

Afghani #1 exhibits typical *indica* traits such as fat, dark leaves and a stocky growth pattern. It also produces an incredible amount of resin, which explains why these plants were chosen for years in their native region in mountainous Afghanistan for hashish production: Their heavy colas, laden with copious resin glands, produce a spicy, exotic taste that tickles the nose and hits fast and strong.

Pure *indicas* are typically high on potency and low on flavor, but the dense buds of Afghani #1 have a distinctly pleasing citrus taste. This strain is perfect for lounging on the couch, but not always the best choice to bring to a party.

Lineage:
Possibly Sensi Seeds'
original Shiva Skunk
[Northern Lights #5 x
Skunk #1]

**Flowering
Time:**
7 to 8 weeks

Contact:
Clone Only

Afghani Bullrider • Jef Tek

According to cannabis folklore, the parent of this strain was spread
around California in the 1980s by a real-life professional bull rider
who worked in a traveling rodeo circus. That original Bullrider was
crossed with an Afghani male in San Diego in the 1990s to produce
the Afghani Bullrider (AB), a potent medicinal strain with interesting
fruity flavors to boot.

The AB was made popular by activists Jef Tek and his wife, Michelle
Rainey. (Michelle, along with Marc Emery and Greg Williams, is part of
the "BC 3"—Canadians from the province of British Columbia, perse-
cuted by the US government for their alleged seed sales.) Throughout
their tribulations, Jef and Michelle have used the AB as their medicine.
Jef tells me he now has a collection of the Afghani Bullrider's progeny,
including the Afberry Bluerider (a.k.a. Sweet #16), an especially sweet
hybrid with a "Blueberry taste and a Hash Plant punch."

Afghani Bullrider starts short and then stretches, flowers re-
markably quickly, and yields plenty of huge buds with high resin content. Jef recommends giving the roots plenty of room to grow. This
strain has that musky flavor and scent well known to *indica* lovers,
and the hash from the AB is pure knockout stuff—heavy on the body
and mind, yet very contemplative and introspective as well.

JEF TEK

 TOP 10

Awards:
• 2nd Place HIGH TIMES Cannabis Cup *Sativa*, 1999
• HIGH TIMES Strain of the Year, 2003

Lineage:
[Colombian x Mexican] x [Thai x Afghani]

Flowering Time:
8 to 9 weeks

Contact:
Serious Seeds, seriousseeds.com

AK-47 • Serious Seeds

HIGH TIMES Seed Bank Hall of Fame inaugural inductee Serious Seeds are known for their unique quiver of five super-stable hybrids that produce Cannabis Cup–winning weed. The legendary AK-47 remains the flagship strain in their decades of strong genetic output.

Sativa-dominant, yet with a tolerably short flowering time and heavy yield, the AK-47 is as easy to grow as she is to love. Commercial cultivators (a.k.a. "cash croppers") prefer clones with stable growing habits; fortunately, cuttings from AK-47 mother plants all perform alike, forming spears of identical thick colas at a level canopy height. Simon has bred AK down to one distinct phenotype that shimmers with resin and produces cannabis that truly qualifies as a "one-hit wonder."

Growers should use plenty of air-cleaning technology to prevent the odor from permeating beyond their grow space. Hash made from AK-47 also reeks with a powerful citrus scent and has a heavy narcotic effect.

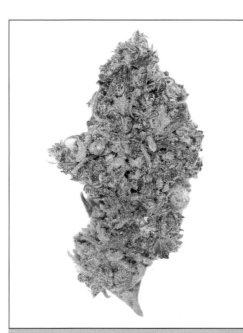

TOP 10

Awards:
HIGH TIMES Top 10
Strain, 2009

Lineage:
Mazar-i-Sharif x
Arcata E-32 Train-
wreck

Flowering Time:
8 to 9 weeks

Contact:
T.H.Seeds,
thseeds.com

A-Train • T.H.Seeds

T.H.Seeds have been at the forefront when it comes to introducing new genetics from California to the Dutch seed trade. As part of that mission, they pollinated the famous Humboldt County clone-only Train-wreck with a heavy-producing Afghani Mazar to create a new strain called A-Train that features the best of both worlds: the fine taste and high of the *sativa*-dominant Trainwreck without the hassles of growing out long, spindly stalks that can't hold themselves up. The Mazar genes also thicken the stems and shorten the gaps between nodes, making for easy-to-trim buds.

Anyone who's tried the original Trainwreck knows the unique flavor and mind-numbing potency of that NorCal staple, and combining those traits with the Afghani Mazar gives A-Train a kick all its own. The initial spicy flavor gives way to a citrus aftertaste, while dry tokes reveal hints of menthol and diesel fuel. *Indica* lovers looking for flavor as well as power will truly enjoy this enticing variety. On a medicinal level, A-Train enhances appetite and lowers ocular pressure, which is particularly important for glaucoma sufferers.

Alaskan Ice • Green House Seeds

Lineage:
White Widow x Pure Haze

Flowering Time:
9 weeks

Contact:
Green House Seeds, greenhouseseeds.nl

A huge hit on the Green House Coffeeshop menu for the past three years, Alaskan Ice combines the best traits of two very different strains, White Widow and Haze. Spicy and "hazy" like a *sativa*, yet frosty and with the complex terpene profile of an *indica*, this strong variety is definitely a future prizewinner.

The Green House's right-hand man Franco tells me: "Arjan developed this strain with a large F1 selection process, followed by a backcrossing to the original selected White Widow father of the F1. The best way to enjoy the Alaskan Ice is in a vaporizer, where all the aromas and terpenes are undisturbed by the combustion process."

Alaskan Ice will grow out stretchier than the Widow for sure, but it's still a heavy feeder. Franco also recommends a timed dosage of magnesium during the resin-production weeks, nearer to the end of the flowering period. Quite resistant to fungus and pests and available in feminized form, Alaskan Ice is a perfect choice for beginners and experts alike.

Alegria • Kiwi Seeds

Lineage:
80% *indica*, 20% *sativa*

Flowering Time:
9 to 10 weeks

Contact:
Kiwi Seeds,
kiwiseeds.com

The Alegria emerged seemingly out of nowhere to win several European cannabis awards for Kiwi Seeds, who are affiliated with the Dampkring coffeeshop. On a trip to Spain in 2003, their breeder was lucky enough to obtain choice seeds from some unique buds and return with them to Holland. The resulting plants were deemed amazing, and so they were promptly pollinated with Kiwi's stable *indica* breeding stock to produce the Alegria now available.

With a scent of fresh lime and pink grapefruit as well as a uniquely nutty aftertaste, Alegria enchants the discriminating connoisseur into true introspection and self-discovery. The intensity of the high has no plateau, allowing artistic types to delve deeper into their most creative places, and medical patients to relieve their bodies and minds.

Alegria exhibits many of the typical *indica* growth characteristics: thick, dark green leaves and tight, spear-shaped colas, as well as a low profile for canopy height. However, this strain also has more of a heady high, a slightly longer flowering time than most *indica*-dominant plants, and exhibits two phenotypes—one finishing around 60 days and the other closer to 75. Both are well worth the wait!

Awards:
- 1st Place HIGH TIMES Cannabis Cup, Best Overall Strains, 2004
- HIGH TIMES Top 10 Strain, 2005

Lineage:
Afghani Hawaiian x Southeast Asian *sativa*

Flowering Time:
11 to 13 weeks

Contact:
Soma Sacred Seeds, somaseeds.nl

Amnesia Haze • Soma Sacred Seeds

Soma's done it again, this time with the appropriately named Amnesia Haze, a spicy mix of Southeast Asian, Jamaican, Afghani and Hawaiian strains that adds hints of pine and black pepper to its fruity bouquet. Truly a mind-bender with a wonderful flavor and aroma, Amnesia Haze is yet another example of the triumphant return of s*ativas* to the cannabis gene pool.

Longer-flowering *sativas* take a great deal of patience to cultivate (some won't show flowers until a month after the blooming period is induced), but the taste and high amply repay the extra investment of time. When growing the Amnesia Haze, go light on fertilizer (preferably organic compost tea and liquid seaweed); Hazes tend to respond poorly to over-fertilization and overwatering, which means it's always best to err on the side of caution. Also, be sure to give the roots room to spread out. After a slow maturation that can drive some growers crazy, you'll be rewarded with some of the most uplifting ganja on the planet, and soon you'll be soaring ever higher with hit after hit of the piney and spicy Amnesia Haze.

AMS • Green House Seeds

Lineage:
Swiss *sativa* x Swiss *indica*

Flowering Time:
8 to 9 weeks

Contact:
Green House Seeds,
greenhouseseeds.nl

The Green House bud-breeding team could easily rest on its laurels after years of award-winning genetics, yet they continue to innovate and produce exceptional hybrids for the worldwide market. Witness their new AMS strain, a *sativa-indica* cross with a sweet, complex taste and a mind/body high that has a strong yet soothing effect. The relaxing smoke boasts a substantial mouthfeel full of rich, spicy notes and a sugary finish.

Growers planting AMS seeds will see fast growth and immediate vigor as their well-lit seedlings develop thick stems with alternating dark and shiny leaves. These young plants exhibit plenty of branching, with the typical conical shape of a Christmas tree and short internodal spacing. Perfect for growing outdoors in the full sun, these plants form strong stalks and branches capable of holding heavy buds as they fill out. Resistance to mold and bud rot are especially sought-after qualities, and in this regard, the AMS never disappoints.

The Green House's Franco recommends being patient and letting these plants ripen through the ninth week for the most complex bouquet and high. He adds: "The flower structure is quite compact, with big, round calyxes and pinkish-brown hairs. The calyx-to-leaf ratio is well balanced, and a slow drying will ensure that all the chlorophyll gets out of the flowers for a sweeter taste."

TOP 10

Awards:
HIGH TIMES Top 10
Strain, 2008

Lineage:
Cannalope Haze x
California Hash Plant

Flowering Time:
9 to 10 weeks

Contact:
DNA Genetics,
dnagenetics.com

Anunnaki • DNA Genetics

Having placed or won in almost every cannabis contest they've ever entered, Don and Aaron of DNA Genetics ("D 'n' A"—get it?) continue to ride high. These SoCal transplants to Holland utilized a California Hash Plant female fertilized by a Cannalope Haze male to create the unique and interesting Anunnaki, a tasty and savory *sativa*-dominant plant rich with the scent of leather, cedar and even hints of coffee.

Tall and lanky, the Anunnaki won't be a tremendous yielder, but her subtle tastes and racy "up" high make this a case of quality over quantity. Indoors, growers should do some severe pruning early on to avoid growing too much lumber (i.e., foot-long distances between each node). For best results, crowd the plants together in a "sea of green" (SOG) system. Also worth keeping in mind: The hash from this strain is some of the tastiest I've ever sampled. So let Anunnaki go the full distance, and it will soon become clear that all *sativa*-dominant strains are *not* created equal.

Awards:
• 2nd Place HIGH TIMES Cannabis Cup *Sativa*, 2004
• 1st Place HIGH TIMES Cannabis Cup People's Cup, 2004
• 1st Place HIGH TIMES Cannabis Cup, Best Overall Strains (Arjan's Ultra Haze #2), 2005
• HIGH TIMES Top 10 Strain, 2005
• 1st Place HIGH TIMES Cannabis Cup, Best Overall Strains (Arjan's Ultra Haze #1), 2006

Lineage:
Nevil's Haze x [Silver Haze x Laotian]

Flowering Time:
11 weeks

Contact:
Green House Seeds, greenhouseseeds.nl

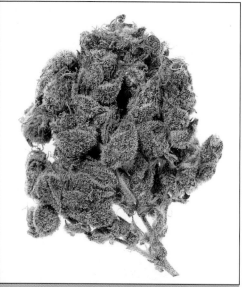

Arjan's Haze #1 • Green House Seeds

The folks at Green House Seeds, the winners of more Cups than any other shop or seed bank, are clearly in the vanguard of Dutch pot genetics. Winning first place in the People's Cup and second place in the Seed Company *Sativa* category at the 2004 Cannabis Cup, Arjan's Haze continues to live up to that reputation. This is a tasty Haze with the long-lasting, uplifting high typical of *sativa*-dominant strains. Arjan's Haze is piney and spicy, with a minty aftertaste. The high has the classic "creeper" characteristics of *sativas*, starting a bit heavy and then evolving into a more subtle and enduring buzz.

Arjan's hard-working right-hand man Franco says: "All over southern Europe, Arjan's Haze #1 is setting the standard for high-yielding *sativas*, with one grower in the Canary Islands of Spain harvesting 1.5 kilograms from a single outdoor plant." (For those folks weak on their metric conversions, that's more than 3 pounds!) Arjan's Haze continues to fill out even in the 11th week of flowering and sometimes develops "dreads"—thin, tubular calyxes that burst forth from the buds late in life.

Awards:
HIGH TIMES Top 10
Strain 2006

Lineage:
Swiss *sativa* x
[Northern Lights #5 x
Haze]

**Flowering
Time:**
10 to 12 weeks

Contact:
Green House Seeds,
greenhouseseeds.nl

Arjan's Strawberry Haze • Green House Seeds

The Green House juggernaut rolls on with the new super-strain called
Arjan's Strawberry Haze. Never shy, Arjan assures me that this spicy
variety will almost certainly add more statuettes to the 30-plus
Cannabis Cups he's already won. It's a flavorful Haze with musky undertones behind a sweet exterior, and a tangy taste that lingers on the
tongue. This *sativa's* effects will surely energize any gathering.

When grown properly, Arjan's Strawberry Haze will exhibit the
long, non-overlapping leaflets typical of an almost pure *sativa*. Internodes grow far apart, giving the plant a stretched-out look; Arjan and
Franco recommend pruning or bending this variety to keep it from
getting too tall and lanky. Also keep in mind that while the ASH isn't a
heavy yielder, its taste and aroma—reeking of ripe strawberries and
other fresh summer fruits—will surely leave you hungry for more.

Awards:
• 1st Place HIGH TIMES Cannabis Cup *Indica*, 2004
• HIGH TIMES Top 10 Strain, 2005

Lineage:
God x [Hawaiian x Purple *Indica*]

Flowering Time:
8 to 10 weeks

Contact:
BC Bud Depot, bcbuddepot.com

BC God Bud (a.k.a. Godbud) • BC Bud Depot

Commercial growers prize *indica* varieties for their potency and large yields, but God Bud also provides great flavor and aroma. Since winning as Best Seed Company *Indica* at the 2004 Cannabis Cup, this frosty selection—already well known in Vancouver—is getting its proper respect worldwide. The dense, crystal-coated BC God Bud has serious bag appeal and packs a hefty punch, with a pungent, nutty odor balanced by a rich, full-flavored smoke.

Matt, the breeder for BC Bud Depot, says: "She's a heavy feeder and can take longer to clone—but once you get it right, there is no stopping her. Yields typically between 2 to 4 ounces per plant in indoor-production setups, and up to 3 pounds per plant outdoors in southern climates. From her density and stickiness to her aroma, taste and medicinal qualities, the God Bud is connoisseur-grade *indica* that will leave everyone wishing for your stash."

I couldn't have put it better myself.

TOP 10

Awards:
HIGH TIMES Top 10
Strain, 2009

Lineage:
BC Mango x KC
Mango

**Flowering
Time:**
7 to 9 weeks

Contact:
BC Bud Depot,
bcbuddepot.com

BC Mango • BC Bud Depot

Strains from western Canada tend to grow reliably and to resist common pests, molds and diseases due to the harsh environment for which they were originally bred. One unique variety from the Great White North is the BC Mango from BC Bud Depot, an *indica*-dominant strain that's great to grow indoors but yields well outside as well, forming super-tight nuggets filled with flavor. This versatile strain makes for a terrific daytime or nighttime smoke with a pleasant yet powerful high.

BC Mango stays short and stocky and tastes similar to mango chutney, with the aroma of ripe, sweet fruit. A perfect strain for the beginner or intermediate cultivator, BC Mango grows uniformly in stature, with little variation among phenotypes. Each plant forms a massive central cola with minimal side branching. Breeder Matt tells me that letting the plants go a little longer than eight weeks adds to their medicinal effects.

TOP 10

Awards:
HIGH TIMES Top 10
Strain 2006

Lineage:
BC God Bud x BC
Sweet Tooth

**Flowering
Time:**
6 to 7 weeks

Contact:
BC Bud Depot.
bcbuddepot.com

BC Sweet God • BC Bud Depot

To create the BC Sweet God, Matt from BC Bud Depot took an exceptionally fast and strong Sweet Tooth male and crossed it into an original selected clone of the 2004 Cannabis Cup winner for Best Seed Company *Indica*, God Bud. Sweet God combines the potency of the God Bud with the faster production and candy flavor of the Sweet Tooth for a heavy-yielding F1 hybrid perfect for commercial growers looking to maximize density.

A real appetite inducer, Sweet God is of special note to medical patients struggling with nausea or vomiting. Improved vigor in this hybrid makes it a hardy plant with a really short finishing time—essential for farmers in chillier climates or higher altitudes. Based out of beautiful Vancouver Island, BC Bud Depot continues to create better and more flavorful *indicas* that produce big, tight and skunky nuggets that are efficient to grow and a pleasure to smoke.

Lineage:
Skunk #1 x Afghani

**Flowering
Time:**
7 to 9 weeks

Contact:
Sensi Seed Bank,
sensiseeds.com

Big Bud • Sensi Seed Bank

Indoor growers looking for dependability should search no further than cannabis-genetics geniuses and HIGH TIMES Seed Bank Hall of Famers Sensi Seeds and their stalwart strain, Big Bud. Originating in the US and brought to Holland in the 1980s, this low-odor production strain has been satisfying cash croppers for years with its invariably steady performance.

The key to the appeal of Big Bud is the strain's consistency. Ken from Sensi Seeds tells me: "Big Bud produces profuse budding sites, short internodal gaps and huge, solid, resin-covered buds. It's also vigorous, uniform and fast-flowering, with modest height gain throughout growth. Many individuals can finish in the shorter flowering time of seven weeks, though the heaviest-yielding ones usually require the full nine weeks. Big Bud has a powerful, mellow effect without being brain-numbing, and a creamy, earthy citrus flavor with skunky undertones." As an added bonus, Big Bud is now newly available in feminized form.

TOP 10

Awards:
HIGH TIMES Top 10
Strain, 2008

Lineage:
BC God Bud x un-
known "black" clone
and backcrossed

**Flowering
Time:**
7 to 8 weeks

Contact:
BC Bud Depot,
bcbuddepot.com

The Black • BC Bud Depot

Following up on their award-winning strain known as the Purps, the BC Bud Depot crew released the Black—a potent and tasty *indica* variety known for her frosty, tight, dark-colored nuggets. She's a heavy feeder, with fan leaves that turn dark purple to almost black as harvest approaches. The Black is definitely a nighttime smoke—truly narcotic, with a stone that hits hard and is especially valued by medical users. Fast-flowering and producing great yields of buds with pure bag appeal, it appears that the Black will be the new Purple for pot connoisseurs.

Matt, the breeder at BC Bud Depot, says: "If there's one plant out there that can exhibit an even more narcotic and medicinal nature than the God Bud, it's our Black. Slightly more astringent and acidic in taste, this musky strain will please all growers interested in dark *indicas*."

Awards:
- 1st Place HIGH TIMES Cannabis Cup *Indica*, 2000
- 1st Place HIGH TIMES Cannabis Cup, Best Overall Strains, 2000
- 3rd Place HIGH TIMES Cannabis Cup *Indica*, 2001
- 2nd Place HIGH TIMES Cannabis Cup, Best Overall Strains, 2001

Blueberry • DJ Short

DJ Short created the original Blueberry in an attempt to tame the wily "Juicy Fruit" Highland Thai and his Purple Thai, while still retaining some of their legendary euphoric highs and fruity flavors. After backcrossing with an Afghani *Indica* male and making careful selections over time, the Blueberry—as well as a whole line of incredible relatives—emerged to impress connoisseurs and growers alike. The potency, odor and taste of this strain rival the world's finest varieties.

The Blueberry stays short and dense, so be sure to vegetate the plants out a bit before inducing flowering. Fan leaves will turn all kinds of beautiful fall colors, and the buds will be tinged with lavender to darker blue pigments. This strain is perfect for the "long cure"—stored in tightly sealed jars for six months or more before smoking, Blueberry ripens into a very intoxicating and complicated flavor profile that's well worth the wait.

Lineage:
Highland Thai or Purple Thai x Afghan *Indica*, or Afghani x [Oaxacan Gold x Chocolate Thai] x Highland Thai

Flowering Time:
6.5 to 7.5 weeks

Contact:
Legends Seeds, legendsseeds.com.

TOP 10

Awards:
• 3rd Place HIGH TIMES Cannabis Cup *Sativa*, 2006
• HIGH TIMES Top 10 Strain, 2006

Lineage:
[Blueberry x Cheese male] x Original UK Cheese

Flowering Time:
8 to 10 weeks

Contact:
Big Buddha Seeds, bigbuddhaseeds.com

Blue Cheese • Big Buddha Seeds

The original legendary UK Cheese meets an elite Blueberry x Cheese male to beget Blue Cheese. The taste and scent of the Blueberry, combined with the raw Afghan power inherent in the Cheese, make for another pungent and potent selection from Big Buddha Seeds, the winner of several Cannabis Cups with multiple British-born strains.

A euphoric high and tart odor and taste are the hallmarks of the Blue Cheese. Big Buddha recommends growing her out in soil for the full spectrum of flavors. The relatively short flowering time and high yield make this variety a perfect choice for a closet or growbox setup. Micro-grown or allowed to flourish in the great outdoors, the feminized Blue Cheese will produce dense nuggets, with some turning purple near the end of flowering. This is a strain destined to pick up some prizes at harvest festivals around the world in the not-too-distant future.

COURTESY OF BIG BUDDHA, HT ARCHIVE

26 HIGH TIMES BOOKS

Blue Dream • Clone Only

Over the past few years, the *sativa*-dominant Blue Dream has become a real dispensary favorite on the West Coast, especially in the Bay Area, where it's a staple at many medical-cannabis collectives. Full-bodied in odor, flavor and high, this colorful strain provides a richness of experience lacking in many other "meds."

Blue Dream also makes a great strain for *indica* lovers wishing to try another route to nirvana. The long-lasting high starts in the head and ends in the body, yet without the sedative effects typical of *indicas*, leaving you fully functional yet pleasantly stoned for a truly expansive and cerebral experience. The incense-like aroma of Blue Dream—capped by a fruity and spicy taste that lingers on the palate—also makes it a perfect strain for making hash. The only problem is that the mites love this plant as much as everybody else does, so stay vigilant and constantly check the undersides of leaves for insects and their damage.

Blue Dynamite • Next Generation Seed Company

TOP 10

Awards:
HIGH TIMES Top 10
Strain, 2007

Lineage:
Dynamite x [Blueberry
x Afghani]

**Flowering
Time:**
6 to 7 weeks

Contact:
Next Generation Seed
Company,
greenlifeseeds.com

As much as we connoisseurs love our *sativas*, we can't neglect the dense and potent *indicas*. Commercial growers in particular prize these branchy and fast-growing strains for their huge yields and abundance of sticky resin. A few years ago, Jay from the Next Generation Seed Company scored his first-ever HIGH TIMES Top 10 Strain with the powerful Blue Dynamite, a wonderful F1 hybrid that's perfect for beginners and pot professionals alike.

Jay created Blue Dynamite by crossing his male Avalon strain (Blueberry x Afghani) with his Dynamite strain (the famous Grapefruit clone from British Columbia). It's a tasty and productive *indica* that turns beautiful hues of blue and purple toward the end of flowering. Jay describes the Blue Dynamite as "a perfect strain for making hash, with amazing taste right down the joint to the end of the roach."

JAY GENERATION

Awards:
2nd Place HIGH
TIMES Cannabis Cup
Indica, 2002

Lineage:
Reclining Buddha x
Afghani Hawaiian

**Flowering
Time:**
9 to 10 weeks

Contact:
Soma Sacred Seeds,
somaseeds.nl

Buddha's Sister • Soma Sacred Seeds

This notable variety from cannabis-breeding legend Soma was originally named the Soma Skunk V+. Since being re-dubbed Buddha's Sister, she's blossomed into a true star on the high-end coffeeshop
market as well as the connoisseur grow scene. The "sour fruit" smell
and candy taste of this Amsterdam stalwart set her apart from the
norm, while her cerebral, thought-provoking high makes for inspired
museum hopping.

Even though she's an *indica*-dominant plant, Buddha's Sister will
grow tall and lanky, with loose, fluffy buds that defy mold and rot. As
usual, Soma recommends an all-organic plant-feeding regimen and
giving it the full 10 weeks. The greasy hash that comes from this strain
lingers on the palate with both tartness and a creamy finish. My es-
teemed mentor, Jorge Cervantes, calls the high "mind-bending" and
praises Buddha's Sister for its mold-resistant qualities as well.

TOP 10

Awards:
HIGH TIMES Top 10
Strain, 2007

Lineage:
Burmese Kush x OG
Kush

Flowering Time:
7 to 8 weeks

Contact:
T.H.Seeds,
thseeds.com

Burmese Kush • T.H.Seeds

T.H.Seeds have earned a stellar reputation for bringing the best of California's genetics to Amsterdam and beyond. This proud tradition continues with their latest offering, the Burmese Kush (lovingly referred to as "Buku"). One of the most resinous strains available at coffeeshops in Holland, Buku is the result of crossing an authentic Burmese Kush with the clone-only OG Kush so well known in the Los Angeles area. As one might expect, the results are super "kushy," with the telltale dark green leaves and unique piney flavor inherent in the Kush family of strains.

Anyone who smokes the real-deal Kush in Cali knows its tart diesel flavor and incredibly euphoric high. Combine those with a short flowering time and easy-to-trim profile, and you'll understand why we're cuckoo for Buku. Adam from T.H.Seeds suggests savoring the instantaneous effects of this strain in a nice clean bong filled with ice-cold water.

Lineage:
G-13 x [Cambodian x Jamaican]

Flowering Time:
13 weeks

Contact:
Soma Sacred Seeds, somaseeds.nl

Cambodian Haze • Soma Sacred Seeds

The legendary breeder Soma, a refugee from the American Drug War who made his way to Holland years ago—single-handedly saving many strains from extinction in the process—continues to provide high-quality seeds as part of his mission to spread this sacred plant and its healing potential to the world. Strains such as Somango, Buddha's Sister and Lavender have firmly established his reputation as a true grower's breeder—one who unfailingly encourages cultivators to use organic techniques to get the best from their plants.

Well known as a *sativa* lover and true cannabis connoisseur, Soma combined Southeast Asian and Jamaican genetics with his legendary G-13 male stock to create Cambodian Haze, a sweet and spicy plant with a long-lasting buzz. Soma tells me that the "Cambo" produces large, long and heavy colas and is a personal favorite of his.

The high from Cambodian Haze must be experienced to be believed. The complex flavors and effects take a little extra time to develop—this Haze finishes in the 13th week of flowering—but it repays your patience with a soaring, euphoric high that seems to have no ceiling.

TOP 10

Awards:
HIGH TIMES Top 10
Strain, 2009

Lineage:
Reclining Buddha x
Sensi Star

**Flowering
Time:**
9 weeks

Contact:
Delta-9 Labs,
delta9labs.com

Canna Sutra • Delta-9 Labs

True connoisseurs know the many positive effects of *sativas*, including their ability to inspire sensual thoughts and feelings. Ed and Harry from Delta-9 Labs crossed the Reclining Buddha with Sensi Star to create the Canna Sutra, a sultry strain that elevates and stimulates the mind (and so much more!), even as the smoke burns soft and smooth and leaves behind a wonderful incense-like smell.

When growing the Canna Sutra, allow a decent amount of space for roots to develop and plenty of room for them to breathe. She'll reward you with a bounty of bodacious buds perfect for a quiet romantic evening with a special friend. A heavy feeder, Canna Sutra is also a little picky about overwatering, preferring "dry feet." Medicinal users take note: Ed tells me that "some users report strong bronchial dilation, which may help to alleviate the symptoms of asthma and related conditions."

Cheese (a.k.a. Big Buddha Cheese) • Big Buddha Seeds

This strain made a big stink at the 2004 Cannabis Cup by placing third in the People's Cup with virtually no promotion or hype. Breeder Big Buddha started by crossing the original British-grown, clone-only Cheese mother with a solid and pure Afghan father, then specially selected their progeny for taste, high and yield. By using selective backcrossing for two years, he was thus able to refine this pungent selection from the UK into a true cannabis contender.

Big Buddha recommends growing Cheese in soilless mix with coco, worm castings, and bat guano to bring out all the piquant and funky flavors. Hash made from Cheese tends to retain much of the strain's unique taste and aroma, while the tight, dense nuggets store well, making them perfect for the long cure.

BRIAN JAHN, HT ARCHIVE

Chemdog • Chemdog—Top Dawg Seeds

Widely believed to be a parent of both New York Sour Diesel and OG Kush, Chemdog has taken the pot-aficionado world by storm. This ridiculously potent strain exhibits a strong diesel-fuel odor that tingles the nose, a tangy flavor replete with hints of cedar-wood shavings and licorice, and a high that will cut through even the thickest fog, making this powerhouse strain a real-deal one-hit wonder.

Completely covered in trichomes, Chemdog ripens into a product so stinky that it must be kept in completely sealed containers at all times. Even while growing, extra care must be taken to contain the plentiful odors. Yields can be quite healthy; Chem himself gets an average of a quarter-pound per plant in 5-gallon buckets indoors. Luckily, the strain is no longer only for Very Important Smokers; rumor has it that, due to a new collaboration with Top Dawg, the real Chemdog family of strains will soon be released in seed form for all growers to enjoy.

TOP 10

Awards:
HIGH TIMES Top 10 Strain, 2006

Lineage:
Chemdog clone

Flowering Time:
8 to 9 weeks

Contact:
Top Dawg Seeds, thcfarmer.com

TOP 10

Awards:
HIGH TIMES Top 10
Strain, 2010

Lineage:
Chemdog (Chem's
Sister pheno)

**Flowering
Time:**
9 to 10 weeks

Contact:
Top Dawg Seeds,
thcfarmer.com

Chem's Sister • Chemdog—Top Dawg Seeds

Though he's become known as the "Midas of Marijuana," Chemdog's original intentions were just to grow the highest-quality pot he could find. Almost 20 years since he popped the seeds from a bag of kind bud purchased on a Dead tour, those rare beans are still causing a ruckus among cannabis aficionados worldwide, and the original Chem's Sister from 1996 was no exception with its powerful and long-lasting high.

The new Chem's Sister, started in 2006 using selfed seeds from the older version, exhibits the same dark orange hairs and "skunky sandalwood" smell, as well as that fruity-candy bite the whole family of genetics is known for. Chem tells me he loves the Sister's mold resistance, noting that "pests don't really like it either." He calls her a "heavy yielder, getting very tall but with even the lower branches getting nuggy."

BRIAN JAHN

Lineage:
Chem D x
San Fernando Valley
OG Kush

Flowering Time:
8 to 10 weeks

Contact:
The Cali Connection,
thecaliconnection.com

Chem Valley Kush • The Cali Connection

The Cali Connection pride themselves on bringing the finest of West Coast genetics to the masses. Breeder Swerve notes that his Chem Valley Kush exemplifies the best of the Kush along with the best of the Chem. He says it smells and tastes like Lemon Pledge, and he couldn't be more right: The odor is almost overpowering, while the rich smoke expands nicely in the lungs.

Growing the Chem Valley Kush requires a bit of effort to get a good yield. When the plants branch out during the vegetative stage, it's time to increase the tops by training them outward. In this way, these incredibly potent Kush plants can become great yielders—they may even need supports for their cola-laden branches as they near maturity. "Screen of green" (ScrOG) growing is recommended as well, using chicken wire or something similar to create a horizontal level to tuck the branches under, thus making use of the entire canopy space.

Awards:
HIGH TIMES Top 10
Strain, 2010

Lineage:
Jack the Ripper x
Trainwreck

**Flowering
Time:**
8 to 9 weeks

Contact:
TGA Genetics,
tgagenetics.com

Chernobyl • Subcool—TGA Genetics

After being gifted the legendary Trainwreck cut on a trip through Cali,
Subcool immediately set about finding a way to incorporate it into the
TGA Genetics breeding program, enlisting his bud Dioxide to pollinate
it with his Jack the Ripper male and study the results. What emerged
was the Chernobyl, a devastatingly beautiful plant with incredible coloring late in life and a taste all its own.

Growers—especially those in the Pacific Northwest—will love the
fact that Chernobyl resists the scourge of powdery mildew. Sub loves
the "unique lime-sherbet smell" and praises Dioxide's ability to
choose special strains for the TGA quiver. Always experimenting and
on the lookout for new gear, Team Green Avenger continues its domi-
nance of dank with the devastatingly powerful and supremely tasty
Chernobyl.

SUBCOOL

Awards:
• 2nd Place HIGH
TIMES Cannabis Cup,
Best Overall Strains,
2007
• HIGH TIMES Top 10
Strain, 2007

Lineage:
Cannalope x Chocolate
Thai

**Flowering
Time:**
9 to 10 weeks

Contact:
DNA Genetics,
dnagenetics.com

Chocolope • DNA Genetics

Anyone who remembers the Chocolate Thai buds that went around in
the 1980s will be thrilled to hear that the DNA Genetics boys have
been hard at work reviving the incredible taste and cerebral high of
that fantastic weed from yesteryear. Don and Aaron sprinkled their
Chocolate Thai female with pollen from their Cannalope male and then
backcrossed the progeny to shorten the flowering time a bit, while still
retaining that unique chocolaty flavor.

This almost pure *sativa* takes a bit longer than some strains to finish flowering, but it yields quite nicely and has great medicinal value.
Unseasoned smokers should beware: Stifled giggles can turn into un-
controllable laughter, and some people even report racing hearts and
paranoia as among the symptoms of overpuffing this strain. One friend
referred to it as a "high-school" high, one that reminded her of her
earliest experiences with cannabis. If that sounds interesting to you,
try some potent and flavorful Chocolope in your garden.

FREEBIE

HT ARCHIVE

Lineage:
Northern Lights x
[Big Bud x Afghani]

**Flowering
Time:**
8 to 9 weeks

Contact:
Serious Seeds,
seriousseeds.com

Chronic • Serious Seeds

One paradox of cannabis growing is that, typically, the more a particular plant yields, the less the quality of the resulting buds. Simon of Serious Seeds has turned this puzzle on its head with his Chronic, a strain that's perfect for commercial growers who want stability and extreme potency from their pot plants, since its extensive branching from one massive central cola ensures a huge yield from every cutting.

Simon says not to top or manipulate Chronic plants as they grow. The dense buds pack on even more girth as they mature, so be sure to dry and cure this strain properly. Simon improved the strain even further in 2000 in order to maintain its consistency. So if you're looking for a plant with a subtly sweet scent and an unmistakable *indica* punch, give the Chronic a shot in your growroom today.

TOP 10

Awards:
HIGH TIMES Top 10
Strain, 2009

Lineage:
Swiss *sativa*, Skunk,
Super Skunk and
Northern Lights

**Flowering
Time:**
9 weeks

Contact:
Green House Seeds,
greenhouseseeds.nl

The Church • Green House Seeds

The most highly awarded company in cannabis just keeps knocking
them out of the park, and they show no signs of ever slowing down.
Originally developed in Switzerland, the Church—Green House Seeds'
combination of a Swiss *sativa*, Skunk, Super Skunk and Northern
Lights—boasts a sweet and flowery flavor with subtle hints of lavender and violet. Growers will love the compact structure and short
stature of the Church. Endorsed by Snoop Dogg himself, this resinous
strain is also renowned for its resistance to mold, making it perfect for
soggy or foggy regions.

When grown out in large containers, these all-feminized seeds develop into round, stocky bushes with very little space between internodes (a sure sign of their *indica*-dominant heritage), while the lateral
side colas will be almost as big as the main top. No matter what their
religious beliefs, discriminating smokers will be happy to worship in
this Church.

Cinderella 99 (a.k.a C-99)
• Dr. Greenthumb

Awards:
HIGH TIMES Top 10
Strain, 2009

Lineage:
Shiva Skunk x Jack
Herer

**Flowering
Time:**
8 to 9 weeks

Contact:
Dr. Greenthumb,
drgreenthumb.com

The legendary Cinderella 99 (a.k.a. C-99 or just the "Cindy" for short) is once again available in seed form for anyone to grow out for themselves. The complex terpene profile gives the nuggets of this strain a lime-pineapple aroma, plenty of back-end flavors and potency to spare—plus the odor while growing barely even smells like cannabis to the untrained nose.

Even though she's slightly on the *sativa* side, C-99 yields exceptionally well, especially outdoors when given enough room to spread her roots. Medical users report that this strain is perfect for treating nausea. Doc, the breeder who tamed the elusive Cindy, tells me that it's "a selection from the most potent we've ever found in our tests with original Cinderella F1 seeds and their progeny. No C-99 we have tested has even come close to the resin production and high THC content on this special plant."

TOP 10

Awards:
HIGH TIMES Top 10
Strain, 2008

Lineage:
Trainwreck x Jasmine

**Flowering
Time:**
7 to 9 weeks

Contact:
Reserva Privada,
dnagenetics.com

Cole Train • Reserva Privada

Several years ago, Don and Aaron from DNA Genetics decided to develop a showcase for some of their favorite medicinal strains from their buddies back home in California. The idea was to take the West Coast's finest private-vintage pot, such as this Top 10 Strain for 2008, and release it to the public through a collective they call Reserva Privada.

Cole Train originated in the Humboldt County area and was created by pollinating the female Jasmine (a mid-'90s Silver Haze hybrid) with a Trainwreck (T4) male. The result tastes like the fabled old-school Colombian genetics treasured by seasoned smokers of yore. A mostly *indica* variety developed amid the mist and fog of coastal California, the Cole Train also resists pests and molds, making it perfect to grow out in harsh or wetter climates.

The Cannabis Cup

Crimea Blue • Barney's Farm

Awards:
2nd Place Cannabis
Cup *Indica,* 2007

Lineage:
Ukrainian Hash Plant
x Blueberry

**Flowering
Time:**
8 to 9 weeks

Contact:
Barney's Farm,
barneysfarm.com

Derry and his team of Barney's Farm bud breeders are constantly on the lookout for unique and eye-opening strains to grow out for the menus at some of Amsterdam's finest coffeeshops. This attention to connoisseur-level detail and quality has resulted in the stabilization of a wonderful new prizewinner called Crimea Blue, a strain with a rare Ukrainian Hash Plant pedigree combined with the popular Blueberry for added flavor and improved complexity.

This *indica*-dominant monster plant's cuttings root fast, respond to flowering induction quickly, and grow into great yielders, producing spear after spear of beautiful buds. Scents of lemon and pine accompany a cerebral, internal high that's perfect for creative or spiritual pursuits. My colleague Nico Escondido, the cultivation editor at HIGH TIMES, reports that Crimea Blue's "recommended medical uses range from muscle-spasm therapy for multiple-sclerosis patients to pain reduction in the neuropathy suffered by HIV/AIDS patients." These days, Crimea Blue seeds are also available in feminized form.

Dannyboy • Subcool—TGA Genetics

Subcool named this sensationally sticky strain in honor of his cherished friend Danny, whose untimely passing in 2000 left a void in his life. This variety is super-frosty, completely covered with trichomes even to the ends of the fan leaves. Flavored very much like sweet-and-sour cherries, Dannyboy has quickly become a connoisseur favorite, with the added distinction that growers love it too.

Among its many desirable characteristics, Dannyboy grows short and wide, with very little stretch after flowering is induced. This strain shows resin early and often and matures very quickly.

Subcool tells me: "Dannyboy is in my top-five favorite smokes. Growers can cut it down as early as 45 days, but it will get larger if you can wait."

Dannyboy is the type of strain that's best explored with a vaporizer in order to truly appreciate its subtleties of flavor. Hints of mango and other ripe fruits combine with the tanginess of the male Taco pheno from the Ortega/C-99 cross. This strain is a moving tribute to a departed brother: *Oh, Dannyboy, the pipes are calling ....*

Lineage:
Killer Queen x [Ortega x C-99]

Flowering Time:
6 to 7 weeks

Contact:
TGA Genetics.
tgagenetics.com

TOP 10

Awards:
HIGH TIMES Top 10
Strain, 2008

Lineage:
Thai x [Mexican x
Colombian]

**Flowering
Time:**
8 to 12 weeks

Contact:
Cannabiogen Seeds,
cannabiogen.com

Destroyer • Cannabiogen

Spain continues to assert its global ganja presence with incredible genetics geared for growers interested in heavy yields of the stickiest
ganja. On a recent visit to Barcelona for the Spannabis Fair, I was
lucky enough to sample the Destroyer, a powerful strain from Cannabiogen, a company long at the forefront of the Spanish sensi surge. It
took them over seven years to backcross this Thai-leaning variety into
something quite special.

Destroyer is an almost pure *sativa* with a mixed heritage (including
some Mexican and Colombian genetics) and the exotic flavors and racy
highs typical of Thai. The expert breeders at Cannabiogen recommend
keeping the roots a bit dry during flowering and going easy on the nutrients (especially nitrogen) throughout growth. The longer you let this plant
flower, the more psychedelic the experience of smoking her becomes. So
be patient with this one—the results will destroy you, but in a good way.

Awards:
HIGH TIMES Top 10
Strain, 2009

Lineage:
NYC Diesel x Lowryder

Flowering Time:
6 to 8 weeks

Contact:
High Bred Seeds,
lowryder.co.uk

Diesel Ryder • The Joint Doctor

Strains that flower automatically no matter what light cycle they're in are all the rage among some growers, and the Joint Doctor has been in the vanguard of this emerging market as the original breeder of Lowryder. Now he's providing the world with feminized auto-flowering for the first time with Diesel Ryder, a cross of the Lowryder with Soma's NYC Diesel, and we're happy to report that the new strain's Diesel heritage gives it the potency that's sometimes lacking in varieties with *ruderalis* traits.

Diesel Ryder typically grows one main cola and begins flowering automatically at three to four weeks. The short overall flowering time makes this strain perfect for high altitudes and northern climates with shorter seasons: You simply plant these seeds and walk away, returning three months later to find short, fully formed bud bushes with long spears of filled-out colas. I'm sure we'll be hearing about these auto-flowering feminized seeds for a long time—and for growers in some extreme climates, they're the only option.

Lineage:
Heirloom *sativa*

Flowering Time:
13 to 14 weeks

Contact:
Barney's Farm,
barneysfarm.com

Dr. Grinspoon • Barney's Farm

This strain was named in honor of noted cannabis researcher and author Dr. Lester Grinspoon, the Harvard Medical School professor whose brilliant advocacy and writing in defense of marijuana spans four decades. Pure *sativas* are a true rarity in ganja genetics, and Dr. Grinspoon is one of the best I've ever sampled that's available in seed form. But be warned: The high is so strong and energetic that it can induce racing hearts and even panic attacks in unsuspecting tokers. Long-lasting and very cerebral, this is a true connoisseur's strain, with medicinal properties that aid in the treatment of depression and nausea.

Dr. Grinspoon is recommended only for expert growers who are interested in creating some truly wonderful head stash. The plants take a very long time to finish, stretching tall and growing small, shiny nuggets all over. Rumor has it that the original seed was found in a block of some of the finest hashish to hit Holland in years, but Derry of Barney's Farm has been keeping its true origins a secret.

Early Girl • Sensi Seed Bank

Growing in northern climates or high altitudes requires compact plants that flower quickly and can withstand harsher conditions. For years, Sensi Seed Bank provided the benchmark for outdoor *indicas* that stay short and stocky with their Early Girl, first released in the 1980s and growing strong ever since.

Cultivating Early Girl is simple indoors or out, as this strain is resistant to most problems, including the dreaded powdery mildew. She's also a perfect strain for a balcony or terrace. Despite Early Girl's short season, potency is not an issue—she has a high that's smooth, clean and long-lasting. Ken from Sensi tells me: "Early Girl exhibits strong branching, with lower pairs bending sharply upwards and sometimes producing colas that rival those on the main stem." Outdoors, she'll be finished in mid-September, before the appearance of frost or bud rot in all but the most extreme climates.

Lineage:
Unknown

Flowering Time:
7 weeks

Contact:
Sensi Seed Bank,
sensiseeds.com

The Cannabis Cup

Awards:
1st Place HIGH TIMES
Cannabis Cup, Bio
(Organic), 1998

Lineage:
[Haze x Super
Skunk] x [Brazilian x
South Indian]

**Flowering
Time:**
8 to 9 weeks

Contact:
Green House Seeds,
greenhouseseeds.nl

El Nino • Green House Seeds

Another elite member of the White family (think White Widow, White Rhino, etc.) from juggernaut Green House Seeds, El Nino caused quite a stir at the 1998 Cannabis Cup, winning first place in the "Bio" (or organic) category and cementing its place in pot-genetics history. Great resin production, versatility in growing conditions, and a strong taste and high ensure that El Nino will grow on and on. She's slightly sweeter than the White Widow, with a peppery *indica* aftertaste.

Green House grower Franco tells me: "The El Nino plant stays bushy and short, with thick leaves, very wide leaflets and short internodes. The stems stay strong and sturdy, without the risk of falling or breaking branches." This strain is great for a "sea of green" (SOG) setup, as it can be crowded together and pruned to fill out empty spaces. El Nino is also a heavy feeder on nutrients, so apply those plant foods liberally.

TOP 10

Awards:
HIGH TIMES Top 10
Strain, 2008

Lineage:
Romulan x Space
Queen

**Flowering
Time:**
8 to 9 weeks

Contact:
TGA Genetics,
tgagenetics.com

The Flav • TGA Genetics

Team Green Avenger, led by cannabis couple Subcool and MzJill, are dedicated in their quest to provide prime medicinal hybrids for patients in need. Their newest release, the Flav, combines Canada's legendary Romulan with the original Space Queen (Romulan x Cinderella 99) for a taste sensation that's hard to beat.

Anyone who's grown or smoked the Romulan knows its intense flavor and yields, and The Flav stays true to that heritage. The phenotypes expressed by these seeds all show significant trichome production and will produce sticky nuggets with that characteristic "ripe to rotting" fruit odor of the real Rom.

Subcool tells me: "The Flav has an exotic flavor like some Far Eastern spice. When grown properly, it also has a slightly grapey floral taste that coats your mouth with an oily residue that lasts." As he points out: "Haven't we all been looking for an *indica* with superior flavor to boot?"

Flo • DJ Short

Lineage:
Afghani x Purple Thai

Flowering Time:
7 to 8 weeks

Contact:
Legends Seeds,
legendsseeds.com

Bred by the same genetic genius behind Blueberry, Old Time Moonshine and Blue Velvet, Flo is known for her soaring high, hashy taste and beautiful fall coloring. Flo is a true rarity—a quick-finishing hybrid with *sativa*-leaning flavors and buzz. Another interesting and fairly unique characteristic is her ability to multi-harvest, meaning that you can start taking buds off at 45 days and then keep doing it for the next few weeks. Remember when growing this strain that she's a light feeder and a bit finicky when the nutrients are too abundant.

Purple hues will come out early with Flo, as well as brilliant oranges and reds. Her flavors vary from earthy and mentholated to a kind of sweet sandalwood with many floral undertones. The high is clear and uplifting, making Flo a perfect daytime weed for a walk in the park or a visit to a museum. The cerebral qualities of this strain are renowned the world over, and DJ Short's name has become synonymous with tasty, potent and unique cannabis varieties.

DJ SHORT

Awards:
2nd Place HIGH TIMES
Cannabis Cup *Indica*,
2006

Lineage:
Thai *sativa* x Dutch
indica

**Flowering
Time:**
8 to 9 weeks

Contact:
Ceres Seeds,
ceresseeds.com

Fruity Thai • Ceres Seeds

Although it's strange to think of a Thai strain as an *indica*, Ceres Seeds have created an original *indica*-dominant variety with real Thai flavor and a relatively short flowering time. Their Fruity Thai hybrid has the retro tropical flavor that many old-timers and Vietnam vets remember as some of the headiest weed of all time. Earthy and woody, with hints of cedar and moist moss along with fruity undertones of lemon and ripe melon, this strain combines the taste and high of Thai weed with the resin production and denseness of a typical *indica*.

The growth patterns mimic *sativas* in some respects, producing one large main cola and thinner, smaller branches below. Fruity Thai is also a low-odor strain while growing, with scents and flavors coming out only toward the very end of the flowering period, as well as throughout the curing process. Plus, her functional high has no ceiling, meaning the more you smoke, the higher you go.

Fucking Incredible • Vancouver Island Seed Company

TOP 10

Cannabis couple Kat and G of VISC have been growing and breeding cannabis for decades. Their years of experience creating strains for the harsh environment of Vancouver Island has resulted in plants that can withstand challenging elements and resist molds and diseases, producing huge colas that dry into the stickiest and stinkiest of buds. The wonderfully (and aptly named) Fucking Incredible is a tasty, *indica*-heavy hybrid with lots of vigor that's both easy to grow and "fucking incredible" to smoke.

G recommends using a slightly higher pH for your soil mix when growing the FI, somewhere closer to 6.8. She's also a great yielder when given the room to branch out. The result of two heavy-duty *indicas* that G spent seven generations stabilizing, Fucking Incredible will satisfy the most demanding *indica* lovers as well as all those medical patients looking for serious pain relief.

Awards:
HIGH TIMES Top 10 Strain, 2008

Lineage:
Indica x *indica* backcross

Flowering Time:
6 to 8 weeks

Contact:
Vancouver Island Seed Company, vancouverseed.com

KAT (2)

Awards:
• 2nd Place HIGH TIMES Cannabis Cup, Best Overall Strains, 2006
• 1st Place HIGH TIMES Cannabis Cup, Best Overall Strains, 2007

Lineage:
G-13 x Hawaiian

Flowering Time:
10 to 11 weeks

Contact:
Barney's Farm,
barneysfarm.com

G-13 Haze • Barney's Farm

Barney's head honcho Derry crossed the legendary G-13 male responsible for many of Amsterdam's finest coffeeshop weeds with a favorite Hawaiian *sativa* to create the G-13 Haze, which promptly won Cup awards two years in a row. Spicy and sweet flavors as well as a stupendous, uplifting high make this *sativa*-dominant plant a real keeper.

G-13 Haze grows short and stocky for a *sativa*, forming dense, highly crystallized buds that fill out into long, firm colas. Remember that slow and steady wins the race with longer-flowering plants, so feed the G-13 Haze minimally and alternate between a mild nutrient solution and plain water. The scent will accumulate as the plant matures, finally resulting in a fragrant "fruit bomb" with a taste of incense and even cardamom. Medicinally speaking, this strain can be used to treat depression, ADD and ADHD. The G-13 Haze is also available in feminized form for farmers who don't dig on growing dudes.

Grape God • Next Generation Seed Company

First developed in the harsh environment of western Canada and now basking in the sunshine of southern Spain, Grape God reveals itself as a connoisseur-quality purple strain. Almost a pure *indica,* its taste, potency and growth make this strain super-special and quite easy to grow out almost anywhere.

A quick finisher, especially in its feminized form, Grape God is perfect for cultivating in the full sun under a greenhouse. Thick, sweet buds begin forming within a week of flowering and continue to fill out, packing on weight and turning all kinds of pretty shades of lavender closer to maturity. My colleague Nico Escondido chose Grape God as a particularly medicinal *indica* in his "Spice of Life" article in the first issue of our newest mag, HIGH TIMES MEDICAL MARIJUANA, and I couldn't agree more with that assessment.

Lineage:
God Bud x Grapefruit

Flowering Time:
6 to 7 weeks

Contact:
Next Generation Seed Company,
greenlifeseeds.com

JAY GENERATION

The Cannabis Cup

Awards:
1st Place HIGH TIMES
Cannabis Cup, Bio
(Organic), 1997

Lineage:
Super Skunk x White
Widow

**Flowering
Time:**
8 to 9 weeks

Contact:
Green House Seeds,
greenhouseseeds.nl

Great White Shark • Green House Seeds

The GWS is one of the finest examples of the White family of strains that began with White Widow in the 1990s. A potent *indica* covered with swollen, glandular trichomes, Great White Shark will meet—and even exceed—the expectations of smokers and growers alike in terms of taste, potency and yield.

I asked the Green House's Franco for some details. He responded: "The plant has a typical *indica* structure, with short and steady internodes and a bushy buildup. The branches are short and strong, and the leaf is round and fat with overlapping leaflets. The edges of the leaflets present a very sharp profile, one that reminds me of the teeth of a shark; hence the name." He and Arjan recommend growing the GWS hydroponically to get the most out of this superlative strain, as well as giving her the full nine weeks of flowering for full potency and flavor. Another added benefit is the high calyx-to-leaf ratio, making this plant a real pleasure to trim.

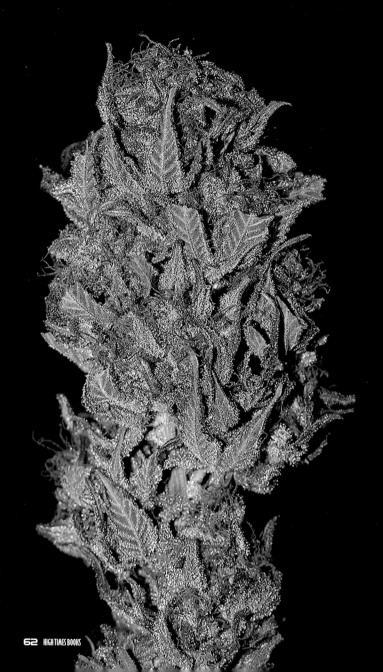

GSPOT • Vancouver Island Seed Company

The Vancouver Island Seed Company, a recent addition to the HIGH TIMES Seed Bank Hall of Fame, consists of married breeders Kat and G. Their new variety, GSPOT (named for G—get it? "G's pot"), is one of the strongest *indica*-dominant selections I've tried from western Canada. With a hashy flavor and stupefying body stone, this strain is perfect for spending long winter nights by the fire with a loved one.

G tells me: "This one's my personal favorite—GSPOT is ass-kicking weed with extreme potency that demands consideration. She grows dense bud upon bud rigid with resins, and her purple-streaked stalks and leaf stems add a visual display as pleasing as her extremely intense flavor." Her many trichomes are great either for vaporizing or for extracting to make some spicy hash. So find the GSPOT sometime soon, and enjoy!

TOP 10

Awards:
HIGH TIMES Top 10 Strain, 2009

Lineage:
Indica x *sativa*

Flowering Time:
6 to 8 weeks

Contact:
Vancouver Island Seed Company, vancouverseed.com

TOP 10

Awards:
HIGH TIMES Top 10
Strain, 2006

Lineage:
Northern Indian
landrace backcross

Flowering Time:
8 to 9 weeks

Contact:
Mandala Seeds,
mandalaseeds.com

Hashberry • Mandala Seeds

This mostly *indica* strain, which made plenty of noise in 2006 and beyond, arrives courtesy of the relatively unknown Mandala Seeds, based out of Spain. Their Hashberry contains rare landrace genetics from Kashmir, a disputed region in the northern part of India where some of the world's best hashish has traditionally been produced. The resulting plants develop heavy and greasy colas whose denseness belies the floral flavor within.

The Hashberry high comes on strong from the very first hit, so if you desire some "couchlock" weed with a truly narcotic stone, look no further. Medical patients prize its healing properties, and growers love the compact and easy-to-manicure profile and inbred heat resistance. I have a feeling the "secret" of Mandala Seeds won't last much longer once a few more people try the amazing selections from these fine folks.

Hash Plant • Sensi Seed Bank

Lineage:
[Hash Plant x Northern Lights #1] x Hash Plant

Flowering Time:
7 weeks

Contact:
Sensi Seed Bank, sensiseeds.com

Typical of the stable Afghani stock chosen for resin production, Sensi Seeds' Hash Plant stays short and squat, with thick stalks and minimal branching. The taste is spicy, hashy and sharp, with the unique bite of a nice piece of dark Afghani hashish. The short flowering time and ease of growth make this strain a true keeper.

Hash Plant can be grown from seed, but she also makes a great mother plant for clones, with each one rooting easily and quickly. Sensi Seeds and other breeders often use the Hash Plant as a building block for their hybrids. Ken from Sensi says: "The buds' structure is, for want of a better term, 'exploded.' They're not airy or feathery and don't really run—it's more that the calyxes, while prolific, aren't squashed tightly against each other as the bud gains mass." He also tells me that, not surprisingly, this strain makes for some excellent hashish.

Awards:
• 1st Place HIGH TIMES Cannabis Cup, Best Overall Strains, 2003
• 3rd Place HIGH TIMES Cannabis Cup *Sativa*, 2003

Lineage:
[Hawaiian Haze x Pure Haze] x Nevil's Haze

Flowering Time:
11 to 12 weeks

Contact:
Green House Seeds, greenhouseseeds.nl

Hawaiian Snow • Green House Seeds

This inspired combination of Southeast Asian genetics (a cross of Laotian with a Hawaiian Haze) resulted in a *sativa* with plenty of flavor and potency. It's a true "creeper" strain, taking 10 to 20 minutes to fully take effect—but when it does, the uplifting high feels inspirational, generating excitement and stimulating the mind and senses. This is a perfect strain for creativity and artistic pursuits.

Franco from Green House Seeds says that it smells like "sweet roasted onion," and I have to agree; I also smell chives and a hint of lilac after grinding up a piece. During growth, the fragrant buds start off looking like tiny puffballs but eventually form into solid and frosty, thickly filled-out spears. Hawaiian Snow exhibits the long, thin leaves typical of long-flowering *sativas* and shouldn't be grown outdoors unless you're certain of no frosts into November. Rot-resistant, she'll eventually start taking on red and purple hues late in life.

TOP 10

Awards:
HIGH TIMES Top 10
Strain, 2010

Lineage:
Haze x *ruderalis*

**Flowering
Time:**
10 to 11 weeks

Contact:
Dinafem,
dinafem-seeds.com

Haze Automatic • Dinafem

Auto-flowering strains are all the rage in Europe and Canada, but they
have yet to take off in the US. But as more and more farmers awaken
to the convenience of growing cannabis plants that start flowering at a
certain height regardless of the light cycle, we'll see these varieties
start to proliferate. Pushing the envelope ever further, Dinafem—a re-
spected and award-winning breeding outfit from Spain—has introduced the world's first auto-flowering Haze hybrid.

Combining the complex *sativa* flavor and psychoactive high of Haze
with a *ruderalis*-tinged strain's ability to bloom automatically, Dinafem has created a truly unique, useful and versatile cannabis variety. In most climates, you can simply plant the feminized seeds any
time the threat of frost isn't an issue, then walk away and return 80
days later to find mature, fully formed flowers ready to trim and dry—
long before the typical harvest season has even started.

Heavy Duty Fruity • T.H.Seeds

Lineage:
Killin' Garberville x
[Mendocino Hash
Plant x Seattle Big
Bud]

**Flowering
Time:**
8 to 9 weeks

Contact:
T.H.Seeds,
thseeds.com

This aptly named strain produces big, colorful buds
perfect for the commercial grower looking for a potent product. The high is almost psychedelic, and
growers call Heavy Duty Fruity a joy to trim as well.
Add to that the bag appeal of huge, sweet and
fruity-flavored nugs, and this one's a ganja
farmer's dream come true.

T.H.Seeds breeder Adam says: "If there's one
plant in our collection that we seem to get the most
praise for, it's surely the HDF. And that's interesting, considering that big yielders are not always the
best in other categories—but we have found that
HDF delivers on taste, effect and yield." He also
cautioned growers to be aware of the extremely
strong odor and stressed the use of air-filtration
equipment for this variety, particularly during flowering.

Lineage:
Indian landrace from the Hindu Kush mountains

Flowering Time:
6 to 7 weeks

Contact:
Sensi Seed Bank, sensiseeds.com

Hindu Kush • Sensi Seed Bank

Pure *indicas* tend to knock people out, but Sensi's famous Hindu Kush has a more desirable zesty quality to it, as well as a rich, hashy smoke that tickles the nose and enlightens the senses. This odiferous strain has a super-short flowering time, coupled with the ablity to start filling out right away for big, fast yields. Great for beginners and experts alike, Hindu Kush is known for its pungent notes of sweetness followed by hints of sandalwood, which distinguish it from the Kush we know and love in the USA.

Ken from Sensi Seeds calls their Hindu Kush "a classic, definitive *indica* sometimes referred to as 'Afghanica,' with the characteristic wide, dark green leaves and strong branching that make it an excellent building block for serious and hobbyist breeders." Indeed, cannabis botanists worldwide use a Sensi Seeds Hindu Kush male in their programs for stability. It also makes terrific hash with an old-school scent and flavor.

The HOG • T.H.Seeds

Awards:
1st Place HIGH TIMES
Cannabis Cup *Indica*,
2002

Lineage:
Kush x Afghani

**Flowering
Time:**
7.5 to 8.5 weeks

Contact:
T.H.Seeds,
thseeds.com

The HOG originally came from Tennesee, moved to Southern Cali, and eventually ended up in the hands of T.H.Seeds breeder Adam in 2003. At first, he wasn't too impressed, but upon flowering this variety out, he realized that the HOG was a power-house strain. *Indica*-dominant, she stays short and fat, with huge, thick, greasy buds that some have described as "too strong," if you can imagine that. Acclaimed cannabis writer and researcher Jorge Cervantes called the HOG's high "classic *indica*— heavy and extraordinarily stony."

Now in his 17th year of creating high-quality can-nabis genetics, Adam reports that "there are Spanish seed companies using our HOG in their breeding pro-grams and winning awards there as well." He also notes that the HOG produces incredible resin for hashmaking and is easy to grow and trim, with thick, glossy fan leaves and a high calyx-to-leaf ratio.

Lineage:
Sweet Pink Grapefruit
x Big Skunk #1

**Flowering
Time:** 9 weeks

Contact:
Next Generation Seed
Company,
greenlifeseeds.com

Island Sweet Skunk •
Next Generation Seed Company

Grown out on Vancouver Island for decades after being developed by
Jordan of the Islands, this *sativa*-dominant sensi staple continues to
wow generation after generation of discerning Canadian tokers. The
ISS's unique flavor and odor—sugary sweet, with a scent that includes
undertones of cedar and cinnamon—keep this tasty treat on the marijuana map, despite her tendency to stretch during growth. The high
can only be described as cerebral and uplifting, perfect for inspiration
during the region's long winters.

When cultivated properly, Island Sweet Skunk yields heavy harvests of trichome-coated, bright orange tops. She's a heavy feeder
early in life, but growers should cut back on the nutrients after a
month or so. Let the stretch work for you by implementing a branch-
training regimen, or use a "screen of green" (ScrOG) approach to
spread the plant out into the available light. Also, be sure to let the ISS
flower the full distance to get the most essential-oil production.

Awards:
3rd Place HIGH
TIMES Cannabis Cup,
Best Overall Strains,
2004

Lineage:
Jack Herer x Super
Skunk

**Flowering
Time:**
9 to 10 weeks

Contact:
Sensi Seed Bank,
sensiseeds.com

Jack Flash • Sensi Seed Bank

Sensi breeder Ken says: "One of two main descendents of our Jack
Herer genotype, Jack Flash was bred to explore the more *indica* side
of this wonderful Haze/Skunk variety. Growers with experience will
detect the Afghani qualities in the background, such as greater bud
density, thick stalks and a hint of sandalwood to the flavor."

Some Jack Flash phenotypes from seed will show a bit more of the
strain's *sativa*-like characteristics, including the typically sharp Haze
odor and flavor. These versions stretch a bit more but are well worth
the extra trouble. In fact, these are the Jack Flash phenos I would recommend keeping for mother plants, since the true joys of the Jack
Herer family of strains are in its complex and interesting tastes and
high. Medical users also tend to prefer these versions.

Awards:
• 1st Place, HIGH TIMES Cannabis Cup *Sativa*, 1999
• HIGH TIMES Top 10 Strain, 2010

Lineage:
Skunk #1 x [Northern Lights #5 x Haze]

Flowering Time:
9 to 10 weeks

Contact:
Sensi Seed Bank, sensiseeds.com

Jack Herer • Sensi Seed Bank

Bred and named in honor of the late, great Jack Herer, noted marijuana activist and author of definitive hemp text *The Emperor Wears No Clothes*, this strain is perfect for real head-stash-quality nuggets with flavor and potency galore. The Sensi Seeds staff's personal favorite—they call it their "Champagne of Strains"—Jack is frosty and bubbly, with an incredible amount of crystals. Amazingly, even the *stems* of these plants have resin glands on them!

Growers will experience several different phenotypes from Jack Herer seeds, and all are fantastic and complex, allowing them to choose the version they like best. All of the related strains—such as Jack Flash, Jack's Cleaner, Jack Candy, Jackie O and Jackie White—are a testament to the strength and beauty of this variety and its versatility in breeding programs. Medical-marijuana patients suffering from anxiety disorders and fibromyalgia report that Jack treats their symptoms well.

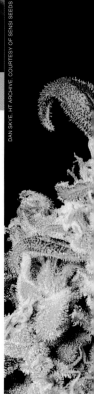

DAN SKYE, HT ARCHIVE; COURTESY OF SENSI SEEDS

Jack the Ripper • Subcool—TGA Genetics

Subcool made my Top 10 Strains list for the first time back in 2006 with his devastating Jack the Ripper, a combination of the legendary Jack's Cleaner (F1) crossed with Space Queen (from Vic High). In Subcool's words, "The lemon tartness of JC has combined with the candy/mango flavor of the Space Queen to create a resinous marvel. This one is the most potent eight-week creeper Haze I've ever smoked."

Grown from seed, the JTR will exhibit shorter node spacing and less stretch when entering the flowering period. Fan leaves are almost completely covered in trichomes, and the buds reek of sour fruit. Smooth, tasty and with a robust high, Jack the Ripper is a true keeper in any mother-plant collection. Also be on the lookout for the very special Pink Lemonade phenotype.

Awards:
HIGH TIMES Top 10 Strain, 2006

Lineage:
Jack's Cleaner F1 x Space Queen

Flowering Time:
8 to 9 weeks

Contact:
TGA Genetics, tgagenetics.com

SUBCOOL (2)

Jillybean • MzJill—TGA Genetics

Female growers seem to have a special connection with their cannabis-plant sisters, and MzJill, Subcool's better half and partner in kind, is no exception. For her first strain release, MzJill crossed their clone-only Orange Velvet female with their trusty Space Queen male to create Jillybean, a euphoric, mood-elevating variety that's easy to grow and exhibits an incredible citrus taste and smell.

Jillybean combines fruity and skunky into a unique and sticky strain that medical users describe as uplifting and happy. She's 70 percent *indica*, so she stays short and stocky and finishes quickly, making her perfect for both "sea of green" (SOG) and "screen of green" (ScrOG) growing. A drop in temperature late in flowering will induce deep burgundy to maroon colors on the leaves of this flavorful and seductive strain. "Some of the best-tasting weed I've ever smoked, and it really does remind me of a candy store. Smoking it makes me laugh and puts me in a better mood," MzJill reports.

Awards:
HIGH TIMES Top 10 Strain, 2007

Lineage:
Orange Velvet x Space Queen

Flowering Time:
8 weeks

Contact:
TGA Genetics, tgagenetics.com

TOP 10

Awards:
HIGH TIMES Top 10
Strain, 2008

Lineage:
Unknown

Flowering Time:
8 to 9 weeks

Contact:
Dutch Passion,
dutch-passion.nl

Jorge's Diamonds #1 • Dutch Passion

In an exciting tribute to Jorge Cervantes, HIGH TIMES' longtime cultivation expert (and my own mentor), the breeding experts at Dutch
Passion Seed Company have created Jorge's Diamonds #1, a strain as
resinous and thought-provoking as the man it's named for.

This *indica*-dominant strain was selected from the 25-year-old
Dutch Passion "research gene pool," and its enticing aroma and incredible taste come from just the right amount of *sativa* genetics
mixed in. Two legends unite to bring the world a new cannabis variety
with a potency that's rivaled only by its amazing flavors and complex
notes. Growing Jorge's Diamonds is also quite a pleasure, since it's
resistant to pests and molds and matures into sweet, fruity-smelling,
berry-flavored buds.

Lineage:
Adonai Kush x
[Cherry Choke x
Strawberry Cough]

**Flowering
Time:**
9 to 10 weeks

Contact:
Kushman Massive
Seeds,
kushmanveganics.com

Jurassic Haze • Kushman Massive Seeds

HIGH TIMES Cultivation Department alumnus (and another of my mentors) Kyle Kushman has finally started his own seed company in order to spread the joy of the many strains he's had the opportunity to work with and refine. When Kyle felt the time was ripe to release his favorite hybrids in seed form, this Jurassic Haze was one of several genetic masterpieces to issue from this sensi superstar.

This *sativa*-dominant monster strain results from crossing the Cherry Choke back to its original mother, the Strawberry Cough. Growing huge, cylindrical colas with an incredible calyx-to-leaf ratio, the Jurassic Haze is one of the highest-yielding *sativas* on the planet. The taste is still fruity, but with heavy, "kushy" undertones from the Adonai Kush father. Super-uplifting with that distinctive Kush high, it's another notable creation from Kushman Massive Seeds.

KYLE KUSHMAN

The Cannabis Cup

Awards:
1st Place HIGH TIMES Cannabis Cup *Sativa*, 2007

Lineage:
OG Kush x Super Silver Haze

Flowering Time:
9 to 10 weeks

Contact:
Apothecary Genetics, apothecarygenetics.com

Kaia Kush • Apothecary Genetics

Apothecary breeder Bret, who created the Kaia Kush, named this strain after his daughter and promptly snagged an elusive Cannabis Cup with it in 2007. Earthy and spicy—and very reminiscent of the Chemdog line of genes—this *sativa*-dominant hybrid has all the lemony-fuel taste and tartness of its predecessors, but with a relatively short flowering time for a strain of such note.

The Kaia Kush is a heavy yielder, packing on weight late into flowering. The abundant and pungent odor can be overpowering, so be sure to use charcoal filtration and whatever else you can find to control the rampant smells. This is the type of weed that can narc you out if you're not careful, so apartment growers especially should take heed. Judging from the reception for this one at many medical dispensaries in California, I'm expecting big things from Apothecary in the future.

The Cannabis Cup

Awards:
•1st Place HIGH TIMES Cannabis Cup *Sativa*, 2000
•3rd Place HIGH TIMES Cannabis Cup *Sativa* (tie), 2002

Lineage:
Cambodian *sativa* x Silver Haze

Flowering Time:
10 to 12 weeks

Contact:
Serious Seeds, seriousseeds.com

Kali Mist • Serious Seeds

I have to admit, this is my favorite *sativa* to smoke in Amsterdam. It's one of the few *sativas* that isn't also a Haze, and the high can only be described as energetic, strong and long-lasting—real head stash with spice. Seek it out in a fine Dutch coffeeshop and you'll realize why Kali Mist has such a buzz about it. I love it as a daytime smoke for its smoothness and potency without a ceiling. This strain is also perfect for treating depression, nausea and migraines.

Of course, like most *sativas* worth growing, this one is a bit tougher to bring to fruition. The somewhat lengthy flowering time and light nutrient needs mean you'll have to treat these long, lanky plants with special care. However, less leaf production means the lower branches get plenty of light, so even the smaller buds fill out and become quite flavorful and dense. Growers in Spain and Canada have also found that Kali Mist resists mold in moist climates.

HT ARCHIVE

COURTESY OF T.H.SEEDS, HT ARCHIVE

Awards:
3rd Place HIGH TIMES Cannabis Cup *Sativa*, 2005

Lineage:
S.A.G.E. x OG Kush

Flowering Time:
9 to 10 weeks

Contact:
T.H.Seeds,
thseeds.com

Kushage • T.H.Seeds

Another sinsemilla stalwart from the T.H.Seeds collection, the Kushage has an epic high—one that hits almost instantly and has both staying power and that familiar Kush headiness. Even beginners will find her easy to grow and work with, resisting many of the common pests and pitfalls that plague first-time farmers. Kushage plants will stretch a bit but fill out nicely, with spicy, piney branches topped with lime-green colas surrounded by dark, waxy leaves.

Adam of T.H.Seeds describes his Kushage for me thusly: "The sandalwood flavor of our S.A.G.E. and the crystal-clear high add an extra boost to the almost addictive buzz of the OG Kush, making this a great plant for the Kush-crazy West Coast of the USA and the Haze lovers of Holland ... truly the best of both worlds!" And he's made it available in feminized form for the first time as well.

FIELD GUIDE TO MARIJUANA STRAINS **87**

Awards:
• 3rd Place HIGH TIMES Cannabis Cup *Indica*, 2004
• 2nd Place HIGH TIMES Cannabis Cup *Indica*, 2005

Lineage:
OG LA Affy x Afghani

Flowering Time:
7 to 8 weeks

Contact:
DNA Genetics, dnagenetics.com

LA Confidential • DNA Genetics

The DNA boys created LA Confidential and instantly won multiple awards worldwide for its unique nutmeg flavor and intense *indica* body high. Medical patients find that the "Connie" is great for relieving pain and insomnia, but recreational users can find it a bit *too* lethargic, sometimes even referring to it as real "couchlock weed."

Growers at every level of skill can produce LA Confidential without much worry, as it's quite mold- and pest-resistant and grows with very little stretch, gaining a foot at most after flowering is induced. "Connie" isn't the biggest yielder in the world, but she will form dark green buds that break up into an extremely rich and flavorful smoke with a truly old-school feel.

Larry OG Kush • The Cali Connection

Lineage:
San Fernando Valley
OG Kush (F3) x Larry
Kush clone

**Flowering
Time:**
9 to 10 weeks

Contact:
The Cali Connection,
thecaliconnection.com

The famed Larry OG cut made the rounds in Southern Cali for years and is an all-time favorite of
Kush lovers everywhere. The archetypal "lemon-
fuel/Pine-Sol funk" (as breeder Swerve perfectly
describes it) is the tip-off that you're dealing with a
real-deal OG cross.

Grown from seed, Larry does some pretty serious stretching after flowering is induced, but
makes up for it with good yields of super-potent
and odiferous pot. Typically producing almond- or
teardrop-shaped calyxes with bright orange hairs,
this strain grows super-frosty, with crystals out to
the ends of the fan leaves (which turn dark purple
as the plants near maturity). The thin, stretched-out branches may
need to be staked for support, and mites love the Larry OG Kush as
well—so stay vigilant and keep checking the undersides of leaves for
damage to catch them early if they happen to attack.

SWERVE

Awards:
• 3rd Place HIGH TIMES Cannabis Cup, Best Overall Strains, 2003
• HIGH TIMES Top 10 Strain, 2006

Lineage:
Thai x Jamaican

Flowering Time:
12 to 14 weeks

Contact:
Barney's Farm, barneysfarm.com

Laughing Buddha • Barney's Farm

The best *sativas* are always worth waiting for, and the Laughing Buddha is no exception: Its combination of Thai and Jamaican genetics makes this strain highly desirable to growers interested in full-flavored and complex bud. The longer flowering time allows the plants to fill out and mature into fluffy white buds that taste fruity and sweet. The intense high produced by this potent *sativa* (from perennial Cannabis Cup winners Barney's Farm) is racy and clear, making it a great daytime smoke full of motivation and energy.

Growing these longer-flowering strains also takes a degree of care. Don't overfeed them, and always err on the side of caution; also, avoid shocking them with light leaks or severe changes in climate. You'll be very happy with the results. The high calyx-to-leaf ratio makes trimming the Laughing Buddha a breeze—simply remove a few fan leaves and the colas are ready for drying and curing.

The Cannabis Cup

Lavender • Soma Sacred Seeds

Awards:
1st Place HIGH TIMES
Cannabis Cup *Indica*,
2005

Lineage:
Super Skunk x Big
Skunk Korean x
Afghani/Hawaiian

**Flowering
Time:**
8 to 9 weeks

Contact:
Soma Sacred Seeds,
somaseeds.nl

Lavender is one of the all-time-best mellow, violet-colored, *indica*-dominant strains available to the public today. By the time she's finished flowering, the leaves will have turned a super-dark purple bordering on black, with bright orange veins running throughout. Dense, winey nuggets of Lavender are a photographer's dream, and she exhibits beautiful fall foliage when ripe. The taste is of plum and pomegranate, well balanced by the hashy afternotes. A dry toke will also reveal hints of an anise or licorice backend.

Lavender plants stretch a bit more than the average *indica*, so be prepared. Her relaxing and sedative high can be a bit much for the unsuspecting toker, but Soma says it's a perfect nighttime or rainy-day smoke, though not recommended for use at parties or prior to activities. For this reason, medical patients looking for help with insomnia should try some Lavender for evening relief.

Legends' Ultimate *Indica* • Legends Seeds

This combination of Breeder Steve's Sweet Tooth (from Spice of Life Seeds) and the infamous Ortega strain from California is a cash cropper's dream. Yet another Canadian genetic triumph, Legends' Ultimate *Indica* from Legends Seeds exhibits all of the archetypal stony *indica* traits with a flavorful, lemony twist. The sugary taste typical of Breeder Steve's work adds sweetness and character to this extremely potent heavy yielder.

Sadly, seeds of this variety are no longer available, but many reliable cuttings remain. Growers who love strong and trustworthy *indicas* would be wise to find a clone of the LUI and hold onto it for dear life. The unique pain-relieving qualities of this strain are of note to medical growers and patients as well, especially those suffering from muscle spasms, back pain and insomnia.

TOP 10

Awards:
HIGH TIMES Top 10 Strain, 2005

Lineage:
Ortega x Sweet Tooth #2

Flowering Time: 7 to 8 weeks

Contact:
Legends Seeds, legendsseeds.com

Awards:
HIGH TIMES Top 10
Strain, 2009

Lineage:
Dutch Skunk x Lemon
Skunk

**Flowering
Time:**
8 to 9 weeks

Contact:
DNA Genetics,
dnagenetics.com

Lemon Skunk • DNA Genetics

The DNA boys took the cannabis-cultivation world by storm several years ago in Amsterdam, and they continue to produce award-winning hybrids with potency and robust flavor. Their new Lemon Skunk, a mostly *sativa* strain specifically selected for its "zesty lemon characteristics," is an easy-to-grow masterpiece of genetic achievement.

Lemon Skunk grows tall, yet boasts a high calyx-to-leaf ratio, making for colas that are easy to trim and a joy to smoke. Sweet, fruity and covered with bright orange hairs, she also packs an impressive punch, with a soaring high that seems to have no ceiling. This citrus strain definitely has pedigree, and harvest-festival awards are sure to follow. Lemon Skunk is also available in feminized form for those interested in growing out only ladies from the start.

Love Potion #1 • Reeferman Seeds

2004's surprise first-place winner in the Seed Company *Sativa* category placed Canadian-bred genetics firmly on the marijuana map. This Santa Marta Colombian/Pacific G-13 cross turns pink as it grows and tastes like sweet lemonade. Even the end of the joint tastes amazing.

The Love Potion's unique *sativa* characteristics make it a little tougher to grow than your average strain, but don't be deterred: This strain will remind older heads of the psychedelic Colombian strains of yore, such as Santa Marta, Punta Roja and the Colombian reds. If you don't know what I'm talking about, do yourself a favor and find out what a true *sativa* from South America has to offer.

The Cannabis Cup — TOP 10

Awards:
- 1st Place HIGH TIMES Cannabis Cup *Sativa*, 2004
- HIGH TIMES Top 10 Strain, 2005

Lineage:
[G-13 x Santa Marta Colombian Gold] x Santa Marta Colombian Gold

Flowering Time:
9 to 10 weeks

Contact:
Reeferman Seeds, thcfarmer.com

Lowryder • The Joint Doctor

Lineage:
William's Wonder or
Northern Lights #2 x
Mexican *ruderalis*

**Flowering
Time:**
6 weeks

Contact:
Joint Doctor,
lowryder.co.uk

This is the one that changed everything: the first commercially available auto-flowering strain that rocked the ganja-growing world by eliminating the vegetative stage of growth altogether!

Lowryder seedlings begin flowering immediately after establishing their first few sets of leaves no matter the light cycle, indoors or out. This allows guerrilla farmers to finish short, stocky spears that are ready to harvest before the choppers even get started—year-round in some climates. (In Spain, the Joint Doctor's new feminized auto-flowering plants are all the rage.)

With its incredibly short life cycle (eight weeks from seed to bud) and discreet profile, it's easy to see Lowryder's appeal for growers. Smokers will appreciate the added potency that's been bred into newer versions such as Diesel Ryder, while breeders will always appreciate the opportunity to experiment with an auto-flowering strain. It's also great for treating severe headaches!

Lineage:
Skunk #1 x Northern Lights #5 (a.k.a. Basic #5)

Flowering Time:
8 weeks

Contact:
Clone only

M-39 • Super Sativa Seed Cub (SSSC)

Released in bean form years ago by one of the oldest (and now long-defunct) seed banks in Holland, the M-39 was touted as a production plant extraordinaire from the very beginning. Heavyweight *indica*-dominant genetics and ease of growth made this hardy strain a staple for Canadian growers from Quebec to Ontario and beyond.

M-39 clones easily, grows incredibly quickly (and with good branching), and finishes with an easy-to-trim profile—all traits that appeal to Canadian cash croppers from coast to coast. Low to the ground and fast to finish, M-39 is perfect for the shorter seasons and harsher conditions of these northern territories.

But beware of imitations! The buds known as "Beasters" are often poorly grown-out M-39 (or even completely different strains mislabeled as M-39). The real deal has that old-school flavor and clean high famil-iar to growers and tokers of a certain age. This strain has also proven valuable in treating medical patients suffering from depression.

Mako Haze • Kiwi Seeds

From far-away New Zealand comes a Haze worth its weight in gold. Kiwi Seeds, affiliated with the incredible Dampkring coffeeshop in Amsterdam, released their Mako Haze a few years back and immediately won the *Sativa* Cup in 2006. The soaring high and uncommonly sweet and spicy flavor were unequaled by any other Haze—and they certainly made the judges sit up and take notice.

Mako Haze grows wispy and lanky, with the long internodal spacing typical of extreme *sativas*, but the final, filled-out spears are completely covered in tiny psychedelic trichomes. Smokers will enjoy one of the strongest yet most intensely pleasing Haze highs they've ever experienced, and true marijuana aficionados will always savor the qualities of unique *sativas* such as the Mako Haze.

HT ARCHIVE

Awards:
3rd Place HIGH
TIMES Cannabis Cup
Indica, 2002

Lineage:
[KC Special Select x
KC-33] x Afghani

**Flowering
Time:**
6 to 7 weeks

Contact:
Attitude Seedbank,
cannabis-seeds-
bank.co.uk

Mango • KC Brains

Longtime Dutch breeders KC Brains won a Cup in 2002 for a tasty, fruit-tinged *indica* with a tropical scent that tingles the nose when smoked. Their signature Mango strain provides a powerful body high and physical stone that's perfect for pain relief and calming spasms in medical patients. Mango is a true "couchlock" weed in every sense of the word, so it's only recommended as a nighttime smoke for recreational users.

Supremely easy to grow, with short, stocky characteristics and a quick flowering time, Mango exhibits very little stretch and, within a week of changing the light cycle, will start stacking flower upon flower of thick, chunky buds. These plants will perform well in soil or hydroponic setups. Remember, this is *not* a motivational smoke—finish up your tasks for the day before firing up some Mango.

Lineage:
Sam Afghan Skunk x
Ortega 15

**Flowering
Time:**
6 to 7 weeks

Contact:
Sensi Seed Bank.
sensiseeds.com

Maple Leaf *Indica* • Sensi Seed Bank

Before the Soviet invasion of Afghanistan in the late 1970s, Mazar-i-
Sharif hashish was known as some of the best in the world. Sensi
Seeds' Maple Leaf *Indica* contains the rare Skunk genes from that era.
Luckily for us, they've preserved these fine Afghani cultivars for use in
hybrids by growers interested in huge harvests of mind-blowing pot.

The short flowering time and heavy yields make the Maple Leaf *Indica* very desirable for indoor farmers. (Indeed, its name derives from
the wideness of the fan leaves.) Short, fat essential-oil glands cover
every available surface, and their sweet maple scent belies a potency
that can take you by storm. Under a microscope, the Maple Leaf *Indica*
buds appear matted with trichomes. Ken from Sensi calls it "one of
our favorite Afghanis—compact and uniform, with moderate lateral
branching, making it ideal for small spaces as well as larger grows."

Lineage:
Maple Leaf *Indica* x Jamaican *sativa*

Flowering Time:
9 weeks

Contact:
Sensi Seed Bank, sensiseeds.com

Marley's Collie • Sensi Seed Bank

Named in honor of the great Bob Marley, the official release of this strain coincided with his widow Rita's historic visit to Amsterdam in 1997 to induct Mr. Tuff Gong himself into the HIGH TIMES Counterculture Hall of Fame. Marley's Collie celebrates the best of Jamaican *sativa* genotypes by pollinating a Jamaican *sativa* female with a Maple Leaf *Indica* male, tamping down those stretchy tendencies a bit. Overall, this combination of Afghani and Caribbean genetics proves hard to resist.

Ken from Sensi elaborates on the characteristics of Marley's Collie: "Lateral branching is vigorous, though arms tend to be quite slender compared to the size of the buds growing on them. Branches may need support toward the end of flowering, as large, spherical colas can form at any node, not just at the top. The buds have a fresh, green and oily aroma with strong notes of fruit and spice as well as a very powerful stone and high."

 TOP 10

Martian Mean Green • DNA Genetics

Awards:
• 1st Place HIGH TIMES Cannabis Cup *Sativa*, 2005
• 3rd Place Cannabis Cup, Best Overall Strains, 2006
• HIGH TIMES Top 10 Strain, 2006

Lineage:
Jamaican Lambsbread x Great White Shark

Flowering Time:
9 to 10 weeks

Contact:
DNA Genetics, dnagenetics.com

DNA Genetics continue to nab award after award with a sensi strain that's completely out of this world. By pollinating a Great White Shark female with a Jamaican Lambsbread male—followed by a grueling selection process—they've created the Martian Mean Green, a hybrid that's 40% *indica* and 60% *sativa*, with a singular smell and potency to match.

John from the Grey Area Coffeeshop describes it as "sweet, minty, with hints of pine, and strong as can be." Martian Mean Green, the winner of the Best Seed Company *Sativa* at the 2005 Cannabis Cup, grows well in hot or cold weather, making it perfect for growers in extreme climates. The DNA boys recommend using organic nutrients and flushing well in the last weeks to get the absolute best from your Green.

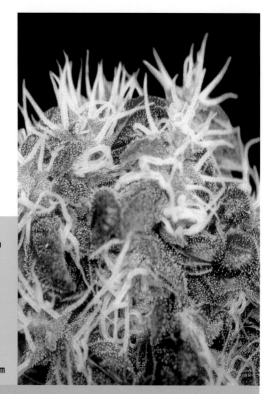

Lineage:
Unknown Alaskan genetics

Flowering Time:
8 to 9 weeks

Contact:
Dr. Greenthumb,
drgreenthumb.com

Matanuska Thunderfuck • Dr. Greenthumb

Originally from the valley north of Anchorage, this legendary (and rumored-to-be-lost) variety from the '70s and '80s returns with a bang thanks to Dr. Greenthumb, a reliable Canadian source of old-school and new-wave genetics. With huge yields of potent colas, the Matanuska Thunderfuck is truly a monster plant when grown outdoors in full sun.

Sativa-dominant in its flavor and punch, yet *indica*-dominant in its growth traits, the Thunderfuck has been known to put veteran smokers on the floor. The sweet and grassy taste followed by a mule-kick high made this the original one-hit wonder of the last frontier—and once you've tried it, you'll know why Alaskan farmers in the know have been growing this one out for years. Lately, the MTF has also been found useful in treating nerve, joint and back pain in medical patients.

COURTESY OF DR. GREENTHUMB

Awards:
2nd Place HIGH TIMES
Cannabis Cup *Indica*,
1999

Lineage:
Afghani x Skunk #1

**Flowering
Time:**
8 to 9 weeks

Contact:
Dutch Passion,
dutch-passion.nl

Mazar • Dutch Passion

Arguably the most potent hashish in the world hails from the Mazar-i-Sharif region in Afghanistan, and strains from this area appeal to *indica* lovers interested in power from their pot. The combo of Afghani and Skunk genes in Dutch Passion's award-winning Mazar gives it a floral fragrance of perfume balanced with the piney odor of cedar and incense.

The long, filled-out tops will turn colorful hues of pink and purple as the Mazar plants mature. Yields reflect the mostly *indica* genetics to a T, with thick, chunky buds covered with plenty of stony trichomes. My colleague in the HIGH TIMES Cultivation Department, Nico Escondido, calls it "a heavily medicinal strain with strong sedating properties, recommended for patients who need muscle relaxation or are looking for help falling asleep at night."

Awards:
• 1st Place HIGH TIMES Cannabis Cup *Indica*, 2003
• 2nd Place HIGH TIMES Cannabis Cup *Indica*, 2004
• HIGH TIMES Top 10 Strain, 2005

Lineage:
G-13 x OG Kush

Flowering Time:
8 to 9 weeks

Contact:
T.H.Seeds, thseeds.com

MK-Ultra • T.H.Seeds

Doug and Adam at T.H.Seeds continue to refine their Cali-tinged collection of great ganja genetics—which includes the S.A.G.E., Bubblegum and Heavy Duty Fruity—by offering up the powerful kick and aroma of MK-Ultra, which immediately brings to mind its OG Kush/G-13 heritage. The Ultra, a flavorful *indica*, is prized by some medical-marijuana patients for providing instant relief. The frosty, resin-coated buds grow into tight nuggets perfect for bong hits or vaporizers.

Adam tells me that they were initially called out by US growers for "breaking the circle of trust and bringing down the legend of the Kush by making it available in seed form. But now, 10-plus years later, Kush is still huge, and there's no stopping the MK." Many consider MK-Ultra to be T.H.Seeds' number one *indica* variety, and it's hard to argue with that assessment once you've grown and smoked it.

Awards:
1st Place HIGH TIMES
Cannabis Cup *Sativa*,
2002

Lineage:
Jack Herer/Haze
backcross

**Flowering
Time:**
8 to 9 weeks

Contact:
Sensi Seed Bank,
sensiseeds.com

Mother's Finest • Sensi Seed Bank

After scoring success with their Jack Herer strain, the breeding
team at Sensi Seeds decided to explore the other phenotypes expressed in this family, and one result of these experiments is their
superb Mother's Finest. This variety combines the best of the *sativa*
traits—including the sweet, piney Haze taste and cerebral high—with
indica's shorter flowering time and preponderance of crystals.

Mother's Finest plants will stretch for the first few weeks of flowering, so keep in mind that vertical space is a must. Clones can be flowered shortly after showing roots. Ken from Sensi says: "Phenotype
variation is limited, with all plants gaining significant height in flowering; however, branching is strong and usually angled upwards at 45
degrees or steeper, allowing large plants to be grown quite close together. Topping generally increases the harvest, especially when done
early in the vegetative stage."

Awards:
• 3rd Place HIGH
TIMES Cannabis Cup
Sativa, 1999
• 2nd Place HIGH
TIMES Cannabis Cup
Sativa, 2005

Lineage:
Unknown male x
White Widow

**Flowering
Time:**
9 weeks

Contact:
Paradise Seeds,
paradise-seeds.com

Nebula • Paradise Seeds

Again and again, Luc and his crew at Paradise Seeds have taken home
prizes for their premium genetics, and the Nebula is no exception. Nick-
named the "Starcloud," this tantalizing variety exemplifies the cerebral
buzz of a *sativa*-dominant strain. A dry toke reveals fruity-sweet flavors,
and the trippy effects begin soon after sparking up, which is why even
seasoned puffers keep gravitating toward the Nebula.

The growth patterns exhibited by this strain make it perfect for
crowding plants together—branches find the open space and fill the
canopy with copious colas, all of them glistening with trichomes. Luc
recommends taking this strain the full distance (65 days or more) for
maximum-sized resin glands. Fully ripened, Nebula will launch you
into outer space!

Awards:
1st Place HIGH TIMES Cannabis Cup, Seeds, 1998

Lineage:
Thai x [Colombian x Northern Lights #5]

Flowering Time:
14 to 16 weeks

Contact:
Green House Seeds, greenhouseseeds.nl

Nevil's Haze • Green House Seeds

An oldie but always a goodie! This one harks back to the days of the legendary breeder Nevil Schoenbottom (sometimes misspelled "Neville"), who found an almost pure Haze and selected back to stabilize its most extreme *sativa* characteristics. In fact, this is the one that started the "Haze Craze."

Arjan and Franco have not only kept this classic strain alive, but they've refined it into one of the most outstanding, long-flowering Hazes in existence. The buzz is physically relaxing, with an inspiring spiritual high.

Growing Nevil's Haze takes time and care. Flowers don't appear until almost a month into the flowering cycle, and the plant will continue to stretch, developing a lot of lumber between each node. The small nuggets fill out and turn white with crystals toward the end of flowering. Outdoors, the branches will stick out at 90-degree angles and find the light in full sun. But if you're a true *sativa* lover, Nevil's Haze is well worth the wait.

Lineage:
Nigerian Silk x
[Northern Lights #5 x
Haze]

Flowering Time:
10 to 11 weeks

Contact:
Top Dawg Seeds,
thcfarmer.com

Nigerian • JJ-NYC—Top Dawg Seeds

African *sativas* hold a special place in the hearts of the "Haze Lovers' Club," and for good reason: Frantic fits of laughter characterize their old-school "up" high (sometimes referred to jokingly as "ampheta-weed"), though real African genetics tend to energize to the point of paranoia in amateur smokers. JJ-NYC, a longtime grower but new-comer on the breeding scene, backcrossed the notorious clone-only Nigerian Silk cutting using a reliable Northern Lights #5/Haze cross to keep those prized African traits intact.

Another strain that requires some patience, the Nigerian grows long and lanky and tends to stretch, but its typical spear-like colas fill out when fed properly, and the yields can be considered decent for a *sativa*. The big reward, however, is in the final product—an electric buzz with no ceiling that can make your heart race. This one is highly recommended for medical patients treating depression, seasonal affective disorder, PTSD and some forms of anxiety—simply prepare yourself mentally to anticipate the rising high and then sit back and enjoy the ride.

Northern Lights #5 x Haze • Sensi Seed Bank

The best hybrids with the most vigor result from crossing two distinctly different strains. One of the first and most successful combinations of two incredible and divergent strains is the legendary Northern Lights #5 x Haze (or NL#5/Haze for short). This strain achieves a perfect balance between these two species of cannabis: The sweetness of the Northern Lights and the tang of the Haze blend into a rich, robust smoke with a near-psychedelic and supremely uplifting high.

Anecdotal evidence indicates that this strain is useful in treating arthritis. Ken from Sensi says that growers can put newly rooted clones or young seedlings of NL#5/Haze into flowering early, but recommends letting them branch out a bit to achieve the full potential of the yield. The stability of this strain makes it perfect as a mother plant or for use in a breeding regimen. NL#5/Haze is now also available in feminized form.

Lineage:
Northern Lights #5 x Haze

Flowering Time:
10 to 11 weeks

Contact:
Sensi Seed Bank, sensiseeds.com

NYC Diesel • Soma Sacred Seeds

Soma continues his metamorphosis into a human/cannabis hybrid with his NYC Diesel, which won an impressive string of awards in the early 2000s, bringing some of the best of New York City to Amsterdam and beyond. After acquiring a Sour Diesel clone from a friend in the "Baked Apple," Soma crossed it with one of his favorite Afghani/Hawaiian males to produce his NYC Diesel, which boasts the scents and flavors of lemongrass, lime and grapefruit—especially ruby-red grapefruit!

Growing NYCD takes patience and a willingness to endure some quirky behavior and fussy nutrient requirements. This *sativa*-dominant plant will stretch for almost a month after you induce flowering, but eventually she'll begin to fill out if treated properly. Go easy on the nitrogen and watch the pH levels carefully; a mild nutrient solution with plain waterings in between are your best bet for success with this superlative Diesel.

Awards:
• 3rd Place HIGH TIMES Cannabis Cup *Sativa*, 2001
• 2nd Place HIGH TIMES Cannabis Cup *Sativa*, 2002
• 2nd Place HIGH TIMES Cannabis Cup, Best Overall Strains, 2002
• 2nd Place HIGH TIMES Cannabis Cup, Best Overall Strains, 2003
• 2nd Place HIGH TIMES Cannabis Cup People's Cup, 2004

Lineage:
Afghani Hawaiian x Sour Diesel clone

Flowering Time:
10 to 12 weeks

Contact:
Soma Sacred Seeds. somaseeds.nl

Lineage:
HP-13 x [Hash Plant
#1 x Double Dawg]

**Flowering
Time:**
8 to 9 weeks

Contact:
Top Dawg Seeds,
thcfarmer.com

NYC HP-13 • JJ-NYC—Top Dawg Seeds

The "HP" in the name stands for Hash Plant, and this one has been an East Coast staple for quite some time. Pungent to the point of being almost acrid, the famous HP-13 that went around New York is the closest thing to the much-celebrated RKS (or Roadkill Skunk) from the 1980s. As the story has it, RKS was the stinkiest and strongest thing going, but somehow became lost to the ages.

Hashy, earthy and skunky in the extreme, JJ-NYC's version of the HP-13 grows short without much branching, making this a great "sea of green" (SOG) strain. It forms popsicle-stick colas of sticky, odifer-ous bud; the aroma while growing is strong and zesty, and the taste of the smoke is very sharp and tart. Older smokers will immediately rec-ognize a smell and flavor they may have thought were gone forever.

Awards:
HIGH TIMES Top 10
Strain, 2005

Lineage:
OG Kush clone

**Flowering
Time:**
8 to 9 weeks

Contact:
Reserva Privada,
dnagenetics.com

OG Kush • Clone Only

This strain has gained an almost mythical status as the foundation of
West Coast genetics. Hippie folklore marks the arrival of superior Afghan
seeds from the Hindu Kush region in the hands of California's growers as
the beginning of a marked transformation in the quality of homegrown
marijuana. This sea change in domestic cannabis cultivation reveals itself
even today in the predominance of Kush traits found among many of the
world's most popular pot varieties. Kush offspring include a number of
Cannabis Cup winners and HIGH TIMES Strains of the Year, including MK-
Ultra and Sour Diesel. Plus, OG Kush offshoots like Bubba Kush and Purple Kush show wonderful promise as future prizewinners.

The DNA Genetics boys started Reserva Privada as a seed bank for
some of their favorite strains being bred out by their buddies in Cali, and
they now have feminized OG Kush seeds available for growers. The yields
aren't huge, but these dense little nuggets pack a legendary punch.

HT ARCHIVE

TOP 10

Old-Time Moonshine • DJ Short

Awards:
HIGH TIMES Top 10 Strain, 2007

Lineage:
Hash Plant x Blueberry

Flowering Time:
7 to 8 weeks

Contact:
Legends Seeds, Legendsseeds.com

Cannabis connoisseurs have long regarded the work of DJ Short as some of the best breeding ever accomplished. He was recently honored as one of the 10 inaugural entrants into the HIGH TIMES Seed Bank Hall of Fame (Oct. '07 HT). Short's Old-Time Moonshine is a mostly *indica* strain that's sticky and sweet, with a deep, musky flavor that's as hashy and earthy as you'd expect from a Hash Plant–influenced Blueberry hybrid.

Red from Legends Seeds says: "The OTM is an F5 IBL [inbred line] from the Blueberry line. The main difference between this one and our Blue Moonshine [the F4 from this line] is the mutant factor: The OTM has a cornucopia of phenotypes that weren't present in the BM. I love the OTM simply for the fact that you'll find mother plants in there that you won't find anywhere else on the market. These ladies also made some of the finest bubble hash I've smoked to date."

 TOP 10

Awards:
• 2nd Place HIGH TIMES Cannabis Cup *Sativa*, 2006
• HIGH TIMES Top 10 Strain, 2007

Lineage:
Unknown

Flowering Time:
8 to 9 weeks

Contact:
Paradise Seeds, paradise-seeds.com

Opium • Paradise Seeds

Luc from Paradise Seeds introduced the strain he calls Opium at the 19th Annual HIGH TIMES Cannabis Cup in 2006 and promptly won second place in the Seed Company *Sativa* category. The creamy fruit-punch flavor cut right through most of the other entries, and this new hybrid will surely be picking up additional awards in the future. The father of this plant is technically actually a mother—a reversed female, a breeding technique that results in female-only seeds.

Opium's huge colas feature an amazing amount of trichomes that activate the senses in a cerebral and visual high that has to be experienced to be believed. Growers will find that Opium benefits from multiple branching for big yields of super-dense buds covered with resin, so use some kind of topping or "fimming" technique to get the most out of her. Opium continues the tradition of great hits from Paradise Seeds.

TOP 10

Pineapple Punch • Flying Dutchmen

Awards:
HIGH TIMES Top 10
Strain, 2008

Lineage:
Skunk #1 x Real McCoy

Flowering Time:
9 to 10 weeks

Contact:
Flying Dutchmen,
flyingdutchmen.com

Since I've always loved the incredible, uplifting and tasty Hawaiian cannabis varieties, and since I really enjoyed Flying Dutchmen's Real McCoy at Coffeeshop Media in Amsterdam, I was very excited to learn of the Pineapple Punch, a cross of a meticulously selected Real McCoy female with a sturdy Skunk #1 male.

The result is a sublime and extremely cerebral taste of the tropics, complete with the unique flavors for which the best *sativa*-dominant hybrids are known. Fruity tastes and scents abound in this flavorful and potent strain. Careful, though—the intense *sativa* elements can cause racing hearts and even paranoia among inexperienced puffers. The rest of us will enjoy their truly powerful tropical punch!

Purple Kush • Clone Only

California has gone "purple crazy," with hundreds of different varieties available in various shades from violet to deep blue. Combining the sweet flavor of the Purps with the lemony power of OG Kush, Purple Kush is a strain that exemplifies the best of both worlds. Strong bag appeal plus increased potency make the PK a perfect hybrid for growers interested in a product that sells itself. Its short, squat stature and heavy harvests don't hurt either.

This clone-only, almost pure *indica* strain has its origins in the Pacific Northwest, but has become increasingly popular and available elsewhere as the rest of the country (and the world) quickly catches up to the aesthetically and spiritually pleasing qualities of these grape-flavored, violet-colored nuggets. Medical patients in particular will appreciate the Purple Kush's deep body stone, which is helpful in treating chronic pain and depression.

Awards:
HIGH TIMES Top 10 Strain, 2006

Lineage:
Hindu Kush x Purple Afghani

Flowering Time:
8 to 9 weeks

Contact:
Clone only

FREEBIE

The Purps • BC Bud Depot

TOP
10
The Cannabis Cup

At the 2004 Cannabis Cup, the guys from BC Bud Depot were gifted the legendary Mendo Purps strain in clone form. Upon returning to Canada, they immediately began working to release stable seeds of this original and fantastic-tasting clone-only variety. The grape-candy favor and deep purple colors are accentuated in this seed release, properly reflecting the Purps' original heritage as one of California's most unique contributions to the cannabis gene pool.

The Purps will yield copious dark nuggets with tremendous bag appeal and an uplifting high that will have you begging for more of Mendocino's finest by way of British Columbia. Joints of the Purps exhibit an almost impossibly candied flavor all the way down to the roach. Dry tokes reveal notes of black cherry, currants and chamomile. BC Bud Depot strikes again with boutique pot for the true aficionado.

Awards:
• 3rd Place HIGH TIMES Cannabis Cup *Sativa*, 2007
• HIGH TIMES Top 10 Strain, 2007
• 3rd Place HIGH TIMES Cannabis Cup *Sativa*, 2009

Lineage:
Purps clone backcross

Flowering Time: 8 weeks

Contact:
BC Bud depot,
bcbuddepot.com

Querkle • TGA Genetics

Lineage:
Space Queen (a.k.a.
Space Dude) x Urkel

**Flowering
Time:**
8 weeks

Contact:
TGA Genetics,
tgagenetics.com

Subcool has unleashed yet another masterpiece of breeding with his new Querkle, a combination of his *sativa*-heavy Space Queen and the *indica*-dominant Urkel, resulting in purple, grape-flavored buds surrounded by fat, dark green leaves. Beautiful plum-colored tops covered in greasy trichomes provide a rich, tasty smoke with a deep-lasting stone.

Try growing Querkle in Subcool's Super Soil (you can find the recipe online) to bring out the most in her odors and flavors. Sub tells me that "Querkle is one of my favorite nighttime *indicas*, with a killer grape taste." One pheno stays short and more purplish, while the other, more *sativa* one has a taller frame and more of an "up" buzz typical of the Space Queen mom. Vegetate for at least a few weeks to get a decent-sized bush and a nice yield of lavender-colored nuggets.

Lineage:
Federation California Romulan Clone x [White Rhino x White Rhino]

Flowering Time:
8 weeks

Contact:
Next Generation Seed Company, greenlifeseeds.com

Romulan • Next Generation Seed Company

British Columbia established itself long ago as the pot paradise of Canada's provinces, and the strain called Romulan led the way. It was first brought to the Vancouver Island area in the '70s by Romulan Joe (a.k.a. Mendocino Joe), and ever since then, local breeders have worked with his rare clones to select for and isolate the classic "Rom" traits.

With a uniquely piney odor and peppery flavor, Romulan represents the finest in *indica*-dominant genetics. These buds are prized by medical patients for their pain-relieving properties and devastatingly powerful couchlock high.

Cultivators love *indicas* for their growth patterns, and the Romulan exhibits all of the classic traits, staying short and stocky, with a good amount of branching and less than a foot of stretch after flowering is induced. Boasting purple stems topped with wide, dark green fan leaves, Romulan packs on weight quickly even in harsh conditions. She will typically turn a beautiful blue tint while ripening, especially in the cold of a Canadian autumn.

TOP 10

Romulan x Hash Plant •
Next Generation Seed Company

Awards:
HIGH TIMES Top 10
Strain, 2009

Lineage:
Romulan x Hash
Plant

**Flowering
Time:**
7 to 8 weeks

Contact:
Next Generation
Seed Company,
greenlifeseeds.com

Medical patients seeking strong sedative effects should look no further than the Romulan x Hash Plant from this outstanding Canadian company, which has been turning out prizewinning genetics for years now. The piney flavor and short flowering time make this a super-desirable variety as well. The frosty "Rommy HP" is also great for making bubble hash—just be sure to smoke it at night, as the hash is a notorious "day wrecker."

Growing this strain couldn't be easier: She'll stay short and stout, with thick branches that withstand the wind while bearing up thick colas of dense *indica* buds. Pest- and mold-resistant as well, this is a great outdoor plant for people in higher altitudes or harsh weather conditions. Set your vaporizer to stun, pack some Romulan x Hash Plant, and get ready for the "trek" of your life!

TOP 10

Awards:
HIGH TIMES Top 10
Strain, 2007

Lineage:
Nepalese landrace
backcross

**Flowering
Time:**
9 to 10 weeks

Contact:
Mandala Seeds,
mandalaseeds.com

Satori • Mandala Seeds

Sativa lovers, rejoice! Breeders Mike and Jasmin of Mandala Seeds
have created one of the finest *sativas* we've ever sampled. Satori combines the wonderful "up" high of a longer-flowering plant with the
production, hardiness and rapid growth typical of shorter, stockier *indicas*. Known for their potent yet affordable strains, Mandala Seeds
produce limited amounts of unique, connoisseur-quality seeds created
from the rare genetics of Nepal and India (where some of the
strongest herb on earth has been grown for centuries).

Mike and Jasmin sell only F1 seeds, which benefit from hybrid
vigor, thus ensuring that plants grown from them exhibit stronger resistance to heat, pests, and the deadly diseases that can be caused by
molds and viruses. The high from the Satori is electric and without any
kind of ceiling; keep on smoking and you continue to soar! This strain
is perfect for those of us with a higher THC tolerance. Medical users
point out Satori's abilities to ease depression and anxiety (unlike some
sativas that can make the heart race). Growers will find her easy to
manicure and a pleasure to cultivate. Take it easy on the nutrients and
let her go the full 10 weeks for complete enlightenment.

Lineage:
Big Sour Holy x Afghani

Flowering Time:
10 to 11 weeks

Contact:
T.H.Seeds,
thseeds.com

COURTESY OF T.H.SEEDS (2)

S.A.G.E. • T.H.Seeds

Adam named this spicy strain *Sativa* Afghani Genetic Equilibrium, but everyone calls it the S.A.G.E. for short. The name couldn't be more apt: S.A.G.E.'s sandalwood scent reminds us of fresh cooking herbs, and the flavor of a joint lingers on the tongue long after smoking. Try exiting the room briefly and then return to relish the rich, pungent smell that the S.A.G.E. leaves behind in her wake.

Adam says, "I have been smoking and loving the S.A.G.E for over 17 years; it's one of my favorites to breed with. There's not enough good things to say about it—if I was left on a desert island, this is ultimately the one plant I would want." The buds swell in size over the last few weeks, so be sure not to take her down too early to get the best flavor and biggest harvest. Medical users will appreciate the S.A.G.E.'s effects in treating mood swings, hepatitis C and PTSD.

Awards:
3rd Place HIGH
TIMES Cannabis Cup
Sativa, 2004

Lineage:
S.A.G.E. x Sour
Diesel

Flowering Time:
8 to 9 weeks

Contact:
T.H.Seeds,
thseeds.com

Sage 'n Sour • T.H.Seeds

T.H.Seeds breeder Adam has been growing out and crossing his
S.A.G.E. with worthy females for over 15 years. Now he's sprinkled his
prized male pollen onto a real Sour Diesel female from NYC to create
the wonderful, award-winning Sage 'n Sour, a beautiful blend of some
of the best of the West with an East Coast powerhouse. This is a plant
that growers and smokers alike rave about.

Sage 'n Sour grows huge when given enough room for the root system to develop, making it perfect for deep-water culture (DWC) hydro-
ponics. Despite the relatively short flowering time, this strain will
swell up tremendously, and its potency level is incredible. Connoisseurs continue to marvel at the complex odors and flavors to be found
within these dense buds.

Awards:
• 1st Place HIGH
TIMES Cannabis Cup
Indica, 1999
• 2nd Place HIGH
TIMES Cannabis Cup
Indica, 2000
• 3rd Place HIGH
TIMES Cannabis Cup
Indica, 2005

Lineage:
Unknown

Flowering Time:
8 weeks

Contact:
Paradise Seeds,
paradise-seeds.com

Sensi Star • Paradise Seeds

This 1999 Cannabis Cup winner is still in the prized collections of many discriminating ganja growers. Minimal branching makes this strain perfect for growing "sea of green" (SOG) style, crowding many short, stocky plants together to maximize space. Once they're covered with frosty THC crystals, the compact buds of this extreme *indica* are both beautiful and intoxicating to behold.

Sensi Star holds a special place in my heart, as it was one of the first hybrids I ever grew from seed years ago. Mother plants of this strain produce perfect clones that root in a timely manner and behave like the prototypical *indica,* producing fat, glossy fan leaves and very short internodal spacing. One of my favorites of all time for indoor growing, Sensi Star will produce thick, dense bushes outdoors in full sun and reach maturity in early October.

TOP 10

Awards:
HIGH TIMES Top 10
Strain, 2005

Lineage:
Mass Superskunk x
Chemdog '91

**Flowering
Time:**
10 to 12 weeks

Contact:
Clone Only

Sour Diesel (a.k.a. East Coast Sour Diesel) • Clone Only

Sour Diesel is without a doubt the world's most expensive pot. With yuppies on Wall Street paying $800 to $1,000 per ounce, no wonder it's so hard to find. Once acquired, however, the real-deal East Coast Sour Diesel justifies its hefty price tag. Powerfully potent, with an unmistakable grapefruit taste and lemony odor, ECSD clearly displays its OG Kush parentage.

Known as a low yielder and notoriously difficult to cultivate, the *sativa*-dominant Sour Diesel takes 70 to 85 days to flower—but is it ever worth it! When flowered at 18 inches tall, the plant will easily grow to 5 feet by the time it's done, making ECSD perfect for extreme training techniques such as the "screen of green" (ScrOG). The strain is clone-only, meaning that seeds of the original mother plant don't exist, but Brett of Apothecary Genetics has backcrossed the original Sour Diesel several times and is close to establishing it as a stabilized IBL (inbred line).

Awards:
• 3rd Place HIGH TIMES Cannabis Cup, Best Overall Strains, 2009
• HIGH TIMES Top 10 Strain, 2010

Lineage:
Sour Diesel x OG Kush

Flowering Time:
9 weeks

Contact:
DNA Genetics, dnagenetics.com

Sour Kush (a.k.a. Headband) • DNA Genetics

East Coast residents familiar with the strain known as Headband will be quite excited to know that the "breeding bros" of DNA Genetics have released a superb version of this famous Diesel/Kush cross. Their Headband won third place at the 2009 HIGH TIMES Cannabis Cup for the Green Place coffeeshop under the name Headband Kush, earning it the first of what will undoubtedly be many more awards.

Don of DNA Genetics tells me that they reversed the OG Kush to pollinate the Sour Diesel, and he assures growers that they'll find a great mother plant out of a pack of 10 beans. Luckily, cloning this strain is easy too, with roots popping out within eight to 10 days of cutting. Headband possesses that familiar diesel-fuel smell and sour lemon taste and starts producing resin glands early and often, exemplifying the best qualities of its elite parentage.

Awards:
HIGH TIMES Top 10
Strain, 2009

Lineage:
Space Queen (a.k.a.
Space Dude) x Tiny
Bomb

**Flowering
Time:**
6.5 to 7.5 weeks

Contact:
TGA Genetics,
tgagenetics.com

Space Bomb • TGA Genetics

Team Green Avenger strikes again in their quest to provide quality genetics for cannabis connoisseurs and medical patients worldwide. The Space Bomb consists of Subcool's Tiny Bomb female fertilized by the Space Dude male to create a super-resinous hybrid. The phenos tend to lean toward their *sativa*-esque C-99 or Romulan heritage, with both growing tall and branchy for decent harvests indoors and out. Subcool says the Space Bomb "tastes like sour candy, with a fruity and prevailing funk, and works well for pain relief."

Space Bomb appeared on the cover of the December 2009 issue of HIGH TIMES, and no wonder—as Subcool told me recently, "It's the most resinous strain I've ever grown and makes large amounts of almost white, full-melt bubble hash." For those wishing to grow true head-stash weed with a super-short flowering time, TGA seeds can be purchased at TGA Genetics, Attitude Seeds and in many dispensaries in California and Colorado.

SUBCOOL

Star Dawg • JJ-NYC—Top Dawg Seeds

From the growers of the real East Coast Sour Diesel comes something even more "diesely"—the Star Dawg, which is quickly replacing Sour D as New York City's favorite smoke. Using heirloom Chemdog genes, longtime East Coast cannabis enthusiast JJ-NYC was able to improve upon an already legendary line of strains with three keeper phenotypes: Star Dawg, Pineapple Diesel and Guava Chem. My particular favorite is the Guava Chem (also known as Guava Diesel), which reeks of sour citrus with strong notes of pine and fuel.

These *indica*-dominant plants will provide a heavy narcotic stone that's great for staying home and playing some video games. JJ-NYC tells me, "Star Dawg was created by crossing Chemdog #4 and Tres Dawg (Chem D x Afghani #1 BX2). It's a fairly easy strain to grow and trim— no topping needed, as she grows big, solid main colas with strong side branches that can be brought up and staked."

Lineage:
Chemdog #4 x Tres Dawg (Chem D x Afghani #1 BX2)

Flowering Time:
9 to 10 weeks

Contact:
Top Dawg Seeds, thcfarmer.com

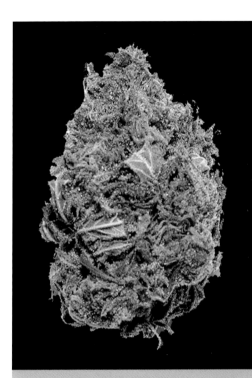

TOP 10

Awards:
HIGH TIMES Top 10
Strain, 2005

Lineage:
Strawberry Fields x
Thai Haze

Flowering Time:
8 to 9 weeks

Contact:
Kushman Massive
Seeds,
kushmanveganics.com

Strawberry Cough • Kyle Kushman—Kushman Massive Seeds

Discovered by Kyle Kushman in Connecticut from an amateur-breeder friend's random Strawberry Fields/Haze cross, Strawberry Cough has quickly attained the status of a legend worldwide. Unique and delicious, the Cough leaves behind a pleasingly sweet sandalwood smell in the room where it's smoked. Those in the know recognize its "hazy" scent immediately, and Kyle tells me he once actually fooled the highway patrol into believing that the odor came from incense.

Cedar dominates the flavor palate when the Cough is smoked or vaporized. As the Kushman says: "The soaring high of the *sativa*-dominant 'Strawbs' has been likened to 'ampheta-weed'—it literally seems to focus my vision on many levels."

Strawberry Cough is another clone-only strain, but a version is available from Dutch Passion in Amsterdam, and will soon be available from Kushman himself via his highly anticipated new seed company.

Awards:
- 1st Place HIGH TIMES Cannabis Cup, Best Overall Strains, 2008
- 1st Place HIGH TIMES Cannabis Cup, Best Overall Strains, 2009
- HIGH TIMES Top 10 Strain, 2010

Lineage:
Lemon Skunk x Super Silver Haze

Flowering Time:
9 to 10 weeks

Contact:
Green House Seeds, greenhouseseeds.nl

Super Lemon Haze • Green House Seeds

Amsterdam's finest coffeeshops pride themselves on their Haze strains, but only the Green House can claim back-to-back wins at the last two HIGH TIMES Cannabis Cups. This citrus-flavored Haze/Skunk hybrid delivers in aroma, taste and potency, and growers will be pleased by its dense growing characteristics, which give higher yields than the typical *sativa*-dominant variety.

The true complexities of Super Lemon Haze are best experienced with a good vaporizer, as the subtle lemon and spice flavors linger on the tongue. My colleague, cultivation editor Nico Escondido, says: "A subtle citrus aroma complements the fuller Haze smell that comes out of each nugget." The high hits the body first and then the head for a long-lasting and pleasant stone. She's a heavy feeder, so don't skimp on the nutrients when growing this variety, which is also available in feminized form.

Awards:
• 1st Place HIGH TIMES Cannabis Cup, Best Overall Strains, 1998
• 1st Place HIGH TIMES Cannabis Cup, Best Overall Strains, 1999
• 3rd Place HIGH TIMES Cannabis Cup *Sativa* (tie), 2002
• 3rd Place HIGH TIMES Cannabis Cup, Best Overall Strains, 2007

Super Silver Haze • Green House Seeds

A pedigree strain with plenty of awards under its belt, Super Silver Haze from Green House Seeds changed the face of Dutch ganja genetics in the late '90s and continues to garner praise and win awards years later. A perfect blend of Skunk, Northern Lights and Haze, the SSH reminds smokers of the best of the coffeeshop Haze hybrids. The odor is spicy and dry, and the strain tastes floral, musky and sweet all at the same time.

When grown, the SSH will exhibit *sativa*-esque qualities, with plenty of stretching and long internodal spacing. The key is to vegetate the plants with plenty of light and keep them short by topping or tying down the branches early in life. Allow lots of space for the roots and you can expect a decent yield that repays your extra efforts. People suffering from nausea or depression report near-miraculous relief with the real Super Silver Haze.

Lineage:
[Northern Lights x Nevil's Haze] x [Skunk x Nevil's Haze]

Flowering Time:
10 weeks

Contact:
Green House Seeds, greenhouseseeds.nl

Super Skunk • Sensi Seed Bank

Lineage:
Skunk #1 x Afghani

Flowering Time:
6 to 7 weeks

Contact:
Sensi Seed Bank,
sensiseeds.com

A throwback to the earliest days of serious cannabis breeding, this combo of Skunk #1 and Afghani provides a perfect example of true hybrid vigor, growing strong, stout plants with thick stems and branches covered in huge buds. Super Skunk is a versatile plant that can be grown indoors or out, in greenhouses and micro-grows alike.

Ken from Sensi says: "Even decades after its release, Super Skunk is still hard to beat. Phenotypes with the largest ball-shaped calyxes are always keepers and usually produce the best resin, yield and flavor." He advises growers to use a variety of odor-control techniques to avoid alerting their entire neighborhood to the presence of their Super Skunks. This strain, now available in feminized form, is an affordable alternative to some of Sensi Seeds' pricier beans.

Awards:
HIGH TIMES Top 10
Strain, 2007

Lineage:
[Oregon Snow male x
Mass Superskunk] x
Bubble Chem [Sagar-
matha Blueberry x
Chem's Sister]

**Flowering
Time:**
8 weeks

Contact:
Top Dawg Seeds,
thcfarmer.com

Super Snowdog • Chemdog—Top Dawg Seeds

The fastest-finishing and sweetest-tasting of all the amazing Chemdog
family of strains, the Super Snowdog just might be the true "holy grail"
of pot varieties as well as an instant connoisseur's choice. Hard to find,
this strain grows incredibly frosty as it finishes and fills out quite nicely
when given enough room. I have to admit that this would be my desert-
island choice if I was ever faced with that daunting decision.

As for the breeding lineage, Chem tells me: "The Snowdog is the
Oregon Snow male crossed with the Mass Superskunk. Then a male
from that cross was chosen to pollinate the Bubble Chem (Chem's Sister x Sagarmatha Blueberry). The result of that cross became the
Super Snowdog." He recommends growing it in at least 5-gallon containers and vegging for a full month to get well over a quarter-pound
per plant.

BRIAN JAHN

Awards:
1st Place HIGH TIMES
Cannabis Cup, Best
Overall Strains, 2001

Lineage:
[Blueberry x Sweet
Pink Grapefruit] x
Grapefruit F1

**Flowering
Time:**
8 weeks

Contact:
Legends Seeds,
legendsseeds.com

Sweet Tooth • Spice of Life—Legends Seeds

Breeder Steve released Sweet Tooth in the mid-'90s to immediate fanfare from his pot-producing peers. Connoisseur cultivators cheered the arrival of a sweet-tasting, *indica*-dominant sinsemilla specimen with a seductively uplifting high. Striking the perfect balance between flavor, potency and production, this lung-tickler quickly became a keeper strain in mother-plant "quivers" from coast to coast.

Sweet Tooth produces fat, lime-green buds with pink hairs and plenty of sticky resins. Grind some up or take a dry toke on a joint to disclose the many tiers of cannabinoid and terpene complexity. Scents of citrus rind, blueberries and watermelon bubblegum hint at the many unique essential oils that make Sweet Tooth especially ideal for hashmaking.

At times, Sweet Tooth plants produce buds so dense that mold and rot can be a problem in humid conditions. The newer backcrossed ST hybrids available from Legends Seeds provide more resistance. Nonetheless, savvy growers always put an emphasis on ventilation indoors, especially with chunky strains like the ST.

Lineage:
San Fernando Valley OG Kush x Tahoe Kush

Flowering Time:
9 to 10 weeks

Contact:
The Cali Connection, thecaliconnection.com

Tahoe OG Kush • The Cali Connection

From eastern Cali comes one of the strongest cannabis varieties of all time, the Tahoe OG Kush—often imitated but never perfected as it has been by breeder Swerve from the Cali Connection, a breeding outfit that has earned much respect for its Kush-heavy stable of strains in seed form. Swerve pollinated the original and legendary Tahoe clone with his San Fernando Valley OG F3 male, and the result adds fuel to the fire for sure.

The Tahoe OG grown from Swerve's seeds produces thick nuggets completely covered in glistening, glandular trichomes, but without the typical hermaphroditic tendencies of many closet-breeding pollen-chuckers' watered-down versions. Medical patients will appreciate the calming properties of the Tahoe OG Kush, which relieves insomnia as well as bodily pains and stress.

SWERVE

Awards:
2nd Place HIGH TIMES Cannabis Cup *Sativa*, 2007

Lineage:
Unknown *indica* x *sativa*

Flowering Time:
9 to 10 weeks

Contact:
Kiwi Seeds, kiwiseeds.com

Tasman Haze • Kiwi Seeds

For too long, the superb strains of New Zealand weren't represented on the worldwide seed market. Luckily, Kiwi Seeds teamed up with the Dampkring coffeeshop to bring us the best that those incredible islands in the Pacific have to offer. Kiwi Seeds burst onto the scene with a second-place *Sativa* Cup win in 2007, and it's easy to see why.

The Tasman Haze yields nice, big chunks of bud with a strong "up" high and pungent odor. Choose one of the shorter phenotypes to grow out for a mother plant and you'll soon be producing some of the most trichome-infested *sativas* I've ever seen. The uniqueness of New Zealand's culture and climate reveals itself perfectly in this one-of-a-kind Haze with a true Kiwi pedigree.

TOP 10

Awards:
HIGH TIMES Top 10 Strain, 2010

Lineage:
Texada Timewarp IBL (inbred line)

Flowering Time:
8 to 9 weeks

Contact:
BC Bud Depot, bcbuddepot.com

Texada Timewarp • BC Bud Depot

This strain is an outdoor legend throughout western Canada and on Vancouver Island in particular. Back in the late 1970s, someone brought a Mexican *sativa* to Texada Island, and thus began the proliferation of Texada Timewarp. Years later, Matt from BC Bud Depot was able to acquire an original clone from the collective responsible for it and continued to work with it year after year to stabilize the line. It was he who told me that its original name was actually "Thymewarp."

Texada Timewarp boasts an earthy, piney taste and a pleasant high that many people find has aphrodisiac qualities. A dry toke reveals hints of lemon and allspice. Outdoor growers in harsh conditions love the TT for its hardy growth patterns as well as its weather resistance. Huge yields of chunky buds before the end of September always ensure a first-class growing season.

Lineage:
Afghani x [Lowland Thai x Mexican/ Colombian]

Flowering Time:
8 to 9 weeks

Contact:
Green House Seeds, greenhouseseeds.nl

Trainwreck • Green House Seeds

The pride of Arcata, CA, the original Trainwreck clone made its way to Amsterdam and into the breeding regimen of the most awarded company in cannabis, Green House Seeds. Arjan and his army have now refined this hard-hitting strain into feminized-seed form and unleashed its famed body high and sage-like flavor upon growers everywhere in the world. They also hope to win plenty of Cannabis Cups with this one.

The most glaring physical property of Trainwreck is its large, tight calyxes covered in greasy resin. Hash made from this strain retains its unique flavor and provides a previously unheard-of level of potency. The terpene profile, featuring higher levels of THC, CBD *and* CBG, make the Trainwreck perfect for treating back, neck and nerve pain as well as the spasms associated with multiple sclerosis.

Awards:
• 2nd Place HIGH TIMES Cannabis Cup, 2009
• HIGH TIMES Top 10 Strain, 2010

Lineage:
Kashmir Hash Plant x Kush

Flowering Time:
9 weeks

Contact:
Barney's Farm.
barneysfarm.com

Vanilla Kush • Barney's Farm

The second-place winner at the 2009 HIGH TIMES Cannabis Cup, Vanilla Kush proves the adage that not all *indica*-dominant strains are created equal. It's hard to nail down the intoxicating scent these buds exhibit upon grinding, which is both complex and varied: Vanilla and sandalwood compete with citrus and lavender as they dance upon the palate. The smoke is full-bodied and sensuous, with the strong medicinal properties associated with heavy-duty Kushes. The higher-than-usual CBD level will especially soothe certain symptoms, such as severe headaches and muscle spasms. In fact, medical patients report immediate relief from smoking or vaporizing it.

When cultivated, the Vanilla Kush boasts dark red hairs surrounding tight, frosty clusters. Even the fan leaves are crystal-coated almost out to the tips, and the buds fill out quite nicely. It's yet another winner from Barney's Farm, and it's also available in feminized form.

Awards:
• HIGH TIMES Top 10 Strain, 2007
• 1st Place HIGH TIMES Medical Cannabis Cup, 2010

Lineage:
Apollo 13 x Space Queen

Flowering Time:
8 weeks

Contact:
TGA Genetics, tgagenetics.com

Vortex • TGA Genetics

Subcool returns with Vortex, his follow-up to Jack the Ripper, one of 2007's Top 10 Strains. For Vortex, Subcool crossed Apollo 13 with Space Queen to produce a potent batch of seeds sure to provide a keeper mother plant with the characteristics of one of two phenos. The Apollo 13–dominant one is called Dynamo and finishes after 58 days; the Space Queen–dominant pheno, dubbed Cosmos, takes a bit longer but grows larger and tastes even fruitier, with interesting sour undertones.

These days, Subcool focuses primarily on plants with medicinal properties, and this one will promote the munchies for those suffering from nausea or otherwise unable to eat. He describes the Vortex as "tasting of sour fruit and pineapple or mango candy. It has a high pistil-to-leaf ratio that makes smoking it a treat, since there's very little leaf on each bud and a thick coating of resin." I've found that Subcool's strains are perfect for vaporizing in the Volcano; their flavor profiles just seem all the more complex and rewarding.

TOP 10

White Berry • Paradise Seeds

Awards:
HIGH TIMES Top 10
Strain, 2008

Lineage:
unknown

**Flowering
Time:**
7 weeks

Contact:
Paradise Seeds,
paradise-seeds.com

Luc and the Paradise Seeds crew have scored pot
points time and time again with their impeccable
breeding efforts, which have produced strong
crosses that will dependably grow into big, chunky
buds. Their *indica*-heavy White Berry is no exception, delivering huge, frosty nuggets covered in trichomes and bursting with flavors both subtle and
pronounced.

The high calyx-to-leaf ratio makes White Berry
easy to trim and absolutely wonderful for hashmaking. It's also a great nighttime smoke, with
soothing qualities that can induce a peaceful, easy
feeling just perfect for sitting on the couch with a
bong and some video games. Medical patients also
highly recommend White Berry for relieving muscle spasms and restless-leg syndrome.

Awards:
1st Place HIGH TIMES Cannabis Cup, 1996

Lineage:
AK-47 x White Widow

Flowering Time:
8 to 9 weeks

Contact:
Serious Seeds, seriousseeds.com

White Russian • Serious Seeds

The White Russian burst onto the scene in the mid-1990s, winning awards for the Dampkring coffeeshop in Amsterdam and raising the profile of pot pioneer Simon of Serious Seeds. Even though it's mostly *indica*, the White Russian provides a cerebral high with complexity and analgesic qualities.

Consistency in her growth characteristics makes this a great production strain for cash croppers. The White Russian's scent is strong, so odor control is a must when growing it indoors. Outside in the full sun, expect a massive harvest of tight, filled-out branches so coated in resin that they literally glisten in the light.

Awards:
1st Place HIGH TIMES Cannabis Cup, Bio (Organic), 1995

Lineage:
Brazilian x Indian

Flowering Time:
8 to 9 weeks

Contact:
Green House Seeds, greenhouseseeds.nl

White Widow • Green House Seeds

This is the strain that, along with Super Silver Haze, put Green House Seeds on the map. Instant success in the 1995 Cannabis Cup led many growers to pursue the White Widow for its tremendous bag appeal: Frosty with trichomes all the way out to the tips of the leaves, White Widow buds look like they've been dipped in diamond dust.

This strain grows compact and dense, with plenty of branching for a short plant. The *indica* qualities are evident in the growth patterns, but the high is something different, starting off really strong and then easing into a cleaner stone for several hours. Hashmaking with the trimmed White Widow leaves produces a pungent soft product saturated with flavorful essential oils.

Willie Nelson • Reeferman Seeds

Awards:
• 1st Place HIGH TIMES Cannabis Cup, Best Overall Strains, 2005
• HIGH TIMES Top 10 Strain, 2006

Lineage:
Vietnamese Black x Highland Nepalese

Flowering Time:
10 to 12 weeks

Contact:
Reeferman Seeds, thcfarmer.com

Reeferman's excellent contributions to the ganja gene pool continue with another triumph, a Vietnamese Black/Highland Nepalese cross that he named in honor of Willie Nelson. The Willie took top honors as the overall winner at the 18th Cannabis Cup, following in the footsteps of Reef's Love Potion #1, the first-place winner in the *sativa* category in 2004 and one of my Strains of the Year for 2006. The soaring high from the Willie Nelson feels downright electric and complements its sweet-and-sour, lemon-tinged flavor perfectly.

Vietnam veterans and old-timers wishing to reminisce should try these genetics for a real blast from the past. True to its Vietnamese heritage, the Willie Nelson packs a cerebral high that can induce panic attacks in unsuspecting amateurs. For the rest of us, it's a truly electrifying buzz with a smoke scented with citrus and cinnamon.

When grown, Willie Nelson will stretch considerably after flowering is induced; it will also exhibit several harvest windows, as the buds continue to pack on girth well after 80 days into the cycle. Don't overdo the nutrient regimen, as this strain is sensitive to overfeeding. Reeferman has done it again with yet another huge advance in his quest for unique pure *sativas*.

Wonderberry • Sagarmatha Seeds

Another member of the inaugural class of the HIGH TIMES Seed Bank Hall of Fame (Oct. '07 HT), Tony, the breeder behind Sagarmatha Seeds, consistently makes careful cannabis selections based in hereditary science and a true grower's instinct. With many prizes under his belt, the fruits of his labor have placed Sagarmatha high on the mountaintops of marijuana breeding history.

Lineage:
Bubbleberry x William's Wonder

Flowering Time:
8 to 9 weeks

Contact:
Sagarmatha Seeds, sagarmatha.nl

   Tony's also known for specializing in the strains of the Pacific Northwest, which is something of a rarity on the Dutch seed scene. The Wonderberry blends his stout Bubbleberry with the legendary William's Wonder to create a flowery variety with notes of orange blossom and lilac. Frosty, trichome-covered nuggets form into very pleasing and easy-to-smoke buds. After harvesting and drying, give this strain a longer cure and a musky sweetness will emerge. Grow it out a bit longer than recommended and beautiful fall colors of deep orange and purple will come out.

TOP 10

Lineage:
S.A.G.E. x Arcata Trainwreck

Flowering Time:
9 weeks

Contact:
T.H.Seeds,
thseeds.com

Wreckage • T.H.Seeds

HIGH TIMES Seed Bank Hall of Fame inaugural inductees T.H.Seeds represent two decades of stupendous genetic achievements, including MK-Ultra, Kushage and A-Train. Now T.H.Seeds have combined their legendary S.A.G.E. (*Sativa* Afghani Genetic Equilibrium) with the famous Arcata Trainwreck for "two great tastes that taste great together." The high is as unique as the odor and flavor, with an uplifting and cerebral effect that every true aficionado desires.

Sativa growers will be happy that the S.A.G.E. genetics have tamed the notoriously stretchy Trainwreck, but you'll still experience some lanky limbs. Luckily, those branches will end in sticky, mentholated colas with that signature spicy sandalwood scent. The last two weeks of growth are a delight to behold, as the tops fill out with clumps of resinous, bulbous bracts. Always remember not to overwater or overfeed the Wreckage. These beans are available in feminized form as well.

Awards:
1st Place HIGH TIMES
Cannabis Cup *Indica*,
2001

Lineage:
Afghani landrace x
Himalayan landrace

**Flowering
Time:**
8 to 9 weeks

Contact:
Sagarmatha Seeds,
sagarmatha.nl

Yumbolt • Sagarmatha Seeds

The extremely sedative Yumbolt from Tony at Sagarmatha Seeds
evokes a lazy summer day in the hills of Northern California's famous
Emerald Triangle. Old-timers from that area will fondly recall its
sweet and fruity flavor profile, with subtle hints of coffee and plums as
well as a stupefying high that is sometimes referred to as being "like a
warm blanket." Medical users will especially take comfort in Yumbolt's muscle-relaxing and pain-relieving qualities while still feeling
uplifted spiritually and creatively. It's not the longest-lasting high, just
a very soothing and balanced one.

Tony was gifted with the original Yumbolt seeds in the 1990s and
promptly began backcrossing for stability, flavor and potency. That
meticulous work led to a stout and hardy, award-winning *indica* covered with glistening trichomes. Strong main stem and branch forma-
tion makes Yumbolt the perfect strain for outdoor or greenhouse
growing, with no staking or trellising necessary.

Lineage:
Afghani x Zero Gravity clone

Flowering Time:
9 to 10 weeks

Contact:
T.H.Seeds,
thseeds.com

Zero Gravity • T.H.Seeds

Last, but certainly not least, is the Zero Gravity from ganja-genetics stalwarts T.H.Seeds. The winners of too many cannabis awards to mention, Adam and Doug both choose to rely on the "Grav" as a daily staple in their smoking regimen. Adam calls it "super-sticky weed with a sweet flavor and very satisfying high."

Its hypnotic effects hit you immediately upon the first toke. Legendary breeders Nevil and Shantibaba originally worked with the ZG as an *indica* parent, but the strain was lost to the ages. Years later, the "Grav" returned as a clone from America, where it had been kept alive by diligent fans of its unique buzz. Adam pollinated this clone-only survivor with a proven Afghani male and then chose the most promising offspring. The resulting hybrid has thin red hairs covering dense nuggets with little leaf to trim.

Acknowledgements

First and foremost, my wife Sarah, whose love and patience endures throughout everything life has in store for us.

My son Alexander (Sasha)—may you grow up happy and free from worry.

My marijuana mentors, Jorge Cervantes, Dr. Lester Grinspoon and Kyle Kushman. Thanks for everything!

My editor, David Bienenstock, for making me sound good, and my book designer, Elise McDonough, for making it look good. And Eric Schoner, for helping track down all the photos. Also, managing editor Natasha Lewin, copy editor Rick Szykowny, and proofreader Mary Jane Gibson.

My publisher, Mary McEvoy, and business manager, Michael Safir, and the rest of the Trans-High Corporation family for publishing this book and enduring my deadline extensions.

My buddy John "Spar," for showing me my first growroom and swinging open the door to so many enlightening possibilities.

The great cannabis writers I've admired and absorbed: Dr. Lester Grinspoon, Jorge Cervantes, David Watson, Robert Connell Clark, Ed Rosenthal, Kayo, Mel Frank, Max Yields, Tom Flowers, Bill Drake, Kyle Kushman, Dr. Julie Holland, Daniel Storm, Dr. Alexander Sumach, Laurence Cherniak, Larry Todd, Jeff Mowta, Logan Edwards, Tom Alexander, Greg Green, Chris Conrad, Jack Herer and Jason King.

Freedom Fighters: R. Keith Stroup, Allen St. Pierre, Michael Kennedy, Valerie Corral, Paul Armentano, Debby Goldsberry, Steve DeAngelo, David Malvo-Levine, Kevin Zeese, Wernard Bruining, Nol Van Shaik, John Sinclair, Stephen and Ina May Gaskin.

My THC colleagues, past and present: Michael Czerhoniak, Nico Escondido, Richard Cusick, Dan Skye, Malcolm MacKinnon, Steven Hager, Frank Max, Natasha Lewin, Bobby Black, Chris Simunek, Craig Coffey, Matt Stang, Big Croppa, Felix Green, Mike Gianakos, Max Abrams, Sheila Avon, Steve Bloom, Ann Marie Dennis, Audrey Bullard, John Veit, John Fortunato, Preston Peet and Valerie Vande Panne.

Photographers: Andre Grossmann, Brian Jahn, Freebie and Lochfoot, Ed Borg, Murphy Green, Jay Generation, Jef Tek, Subcool, Dan Skye, DJ Short, Kat, Swerve, Kyle Kushman, plus all the unsung photographers who shot the photos.

My contributors over the years: Nebu, J.C. Stitch, BOG, Chimera, Crazy Composer, David Strange, StinkBud, Mike Spears, South Bay Ray, British Hempire, Trichome Tech, Subcool, MzJill, Eric Biksa and Dark Cycle.

Everyone who inspired or helped out with this book: Sam Skunkman from Sacred Seeds; Ben, Alan, Ravi and Ken from Sensi Seeds; Nevil from the Seed Bank/SSSC; Arjan and Franco from Green House Seeds; Derry from Barney's Farm; Adam and Doug from T.H.Seeds; Simon from Serious Seeds; Luc and "Ali Baba" from Paradise; Don and Aaron from DNA Genetics; Reeferman from Reeferman Seeds; Subcool and MzJill of TGA; Jef Tek; Kiwi Seeds; Soma from Soma Sacred Seeds; Matt from BC Bud Depot; Big Buddha, Greg and Kat from VISC; Jay from Next Generation Seed Company; Ed and Harry from Delta-9 Labs; Chemdog from Top Dawg Seeds; JJ-NYC from Top Dawg Seeds; Swerve from the Cali Connection; Dr. Greenthumb; Cannabiogen; The Joint Doctor; DJ Short; Ceres Seeds; Bonguru Seeds; Mike and Jasmin from Mandala Seeds; Henk from Dutch Passion; Brett and Jeannette from Apothecary Seeds; Shiloh Massive from Kushman Massive Seeds; Red from Legends Seeds; KC Brains; Eddy from Flying Dutchman; Breeder Steve from Spice of Life; Tony from Sagarmatha Seeds; and Karra Heywood from Van City Seeds.

And there's more: Balta, Hugo, David and Maria in España, DaddyHaze Shawn and Molly, Bubbleman, Sita, Karen, Lorna from Cannabis College, Michka, Mila from Pollinator, Shantibaba, Kevin Booth, Chris Bliss, Papers and Disco, Jose, Caesar, Tarren and the whole BC Northern Lights crew, Jacks Buds and Felicia, EZ-Gene, Haz, Igor Rakuz, DJ Jacques, React Juice, Star David from Lotus Sound, Dao, Popeye Jason, Rob Cantrell, Empire State NORML, "Mojito Man" Junius, The Bonghitters, Louie South Shore, Outkastt and TOH, Reggie Noble and Tariq, Rob Key, Sarah Bambú, Scooter, Wray and Talia, Kid Cudi, Dres from Black Sheep, Bill "Spaceman" Lee, Eric Bobo, my brothers; Ilya and Boris, Mom and Leonid, Jimi V., Hempie Chef of Shasta, Jefe from Aqualab, Derek Botanical, Helmer and Chron Jon.

In Memoriam:

Eagle Bill, Peter McWilliams, Dr. Tod Mikuriya, Gaspar Fraga, Old Ed, Tom Flowers, Carl Sagan, Dr. Jay Robert Cavanaugh, Alex of LMN, Michelle Rainey, Mary Powers, Cheryl Miller, Robert Jasper Grootveld, Robin Prosser, Jonathan Magbie, Donald Scott, Patrick Dorismond, Jack Herer, Peter Tosh, Bob Marley, Dennis Brown, Bill Hicks, Louis Armstrong, Robert Altman, Lee Bridges, Lenny Bruce, George Carlin, Jerry Garcia, Allen Ginsberg, John Lennon and Richard Pryor.

Index to Field Guide Strains & Seed Banks

Notes

Notes

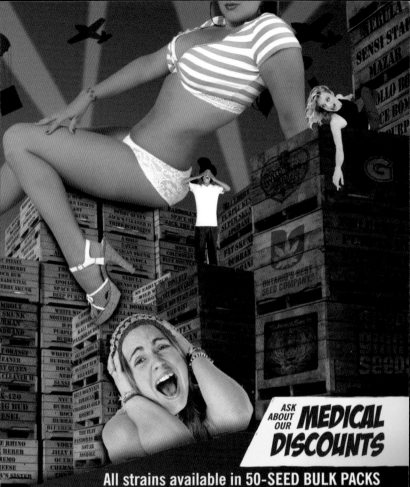

ASK ABOUT OUR **MEDICAL DISCOUNTS**

All strains available in 50-SEED BULK PACKS

CALL FOR PRICING AND FREE DELIVERY

SHOP IN PERSON IN A SAFE ENVIRONMENT

3351 Lake Shore Blvd W - Toronto, ON M8W 1N1

MON to SAT 10am - 7pm | SUN 10am - 4:20pm

Directions: Take QEW Toronto to Cawthra Rd exit, then south on Cawthra to Lakeshore Blvd.
Go east on Lake Shore Blvd for 5 miles. Look out for the neon '420' sign on the south side of the street.

 Canadian owned and operated.

☠️☠️☠️ TO ALL WANNABES ☠️☠️☠️

ACQUISITION OF LIVE CANNABIS SEEDS IS ILLEGAL IN THE UNITED STATES
PAYABLE IN US DOLLARS FROM ANYWHERE IN THE WORLD

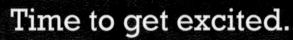

WARNING
KILLER STRAINS

BARNEY'S FARM  LSD	**JOINT DOCTOR**  EASYRYDER	**GREENHOUSE SEEDS**  SUPER LEMON HAZE	**G13**  PINEAPPLE EXPRESS
BARNEY'S FARM  VANILLA KUSH	**TGA SUBCOOL**  QUERKLE	**JOINT DOCTOR**  DIESEL RYDER	**BIG BUDDHA**  BLUE CHEESE
RESERVA PRIVADA  HEADBAND	**SERIOUS SEEDS**  WHITE RUSSIAN	**RESERVA PRIVADA**  OG KUSH	**BARNEY'S FARM**  BLUE CHEESE
SERIOUS SEEDS  AK47	**GREENHOUSE SEEDS**  BUBBA KUSH	**DNA GENETICS**  CHOCOLOPE	**TGA SUBCOOL**  JILLY BEAN

WARNING
KILLER STRAINS